M000203779

The Book of **Bill**

Other Books by Tom Crisp
The Book of Bob

The Book of

Bill

Choice Words
Memorable Men

Edited by Tom Crisp

**Andrews McMeel
Publishing, LLC**

Kansas City

The Book of Bill copyright © 2009 by Tom Crisp.
All rights reserved. Printed in the United States
of America. No part of this book may be used or
reproduced in any manner whatsoever without
written permission except in the case of reprints
in the context of reviews. For information, write
Andrews McMeel Publishing, LLC, an Andrews
McMeel Universal company, 1130 Walnut Street,
Kansas City, Missouri 64106.

ISBN-13: 978-0-7407-7912-1
ISBN-10: 0-7407-7912-5

Library of Congress Control Number: 2008935742

09 10 11 12 13 RR2 10 9 8 7 6 5 4 3 2 1

www.andrewsmcmeel.com

Attention: Schools and Businesses

Andrews McMeel books are available at quantity
discounts with bulk purchase for educational,
business, or sales promotional use. For information,
please write to: Special Sales Department, Andrews
McMeel Publishing, LLC, 1130 Walnut Street,
Kansas City, Missouri 64106.

Contents

Introduction

History records a twelfth-century event in Normandy, where Henry the Young King (not to be confused with his pop, England's Henry II) held a Christmas court for all the knights of his realm. Festivities were complicated when more than a hundred lords, all named William, locked themselves into a banquet hall, refusing to admit any knight otherwise named. We don't know if the expression "bill of fare" was born that night, but it's a sweet idea.

It was the Norman Conquest in 1066, led, of course, by William the Conqueror, that brought the name to the English-speaking isles. The origin of the name is Germanic, via Wilhelm, which is made of two Old German words: *wil*, for will or desire; and *helm*, for helmet. Who wouldn't desire a helmet, if he had to fight a battalion of knights to get some dinner?

In the western world the name has been going strong the past millennium. Not only do Williams, Bills, and Willys count for about 4.5 million American men (fourth overall), but the surname Williams is the third most common in the United States and fourth in the United Kingdom.

William is a noble name—and a versatile one, with a friendly Will, a roughhousing Billy, and a no-fuss Bill in the family. He speaks a dozen languages: he's Willem and Liam, Guillaume and Guillermo.

Who is he? P. G. Wodehouse and Oscar Hammerstein's lyric to Jerome Kern's classic "Bill" says it succinctly: "He's just my Bill, an ordinary boy . . . " or an ordinary rock star or president.

The ability to quote
is a serviceable
substitute for wit.

W. Somerset Maugham

The Book of **Bill**

one

Love That Bill

I never expected to see the day when girls get sunburned in the places they do now.

Will Rogers, 1879–1935
humorist/actor

See, how she leans her cheek upon her hand!
O that I were a glove upon that hand,
That I might touch that cheek!

Romeo and Juliet
William Shakespeare, 1564–1616
dramatist/poet

In Hollywood, the women are all peaches. It makes one long for an apple occasionally.

> **W. Somerset Maugham,** 1874–1965
> writer/dramatist

Her hair was bleached, her eyebrows penciled, her lips painted, her cheeks rouged, her eyes belladonnaed, her nose powdered, and when she entered the car with him, even her mind was made up.

> *Captain Billy's Whiz Bang, July 1924*
> **Wilford Hamilton "Captain Billy" Fawcett,** 1885–1940
> publisher

Those who restrain desire, do so because theirs is weak enough to be restrained.

> **William Blake,** 1757–1827
> artist/poet

A very beautiful woman hardly ever leaves a clear-cut impression of features and shape in the memory: usually there remains only an aura of living colour.

William Bolitho, 1890–1930
writer

Never try to impress a woman, because if you do she'll expect you to keep up to the standard for the rest of your life.

W. C. Fields, 1880–1946
actor/comedian

She's one of the finest girls to come out of Kansas. But I often wish she'd go back there.

about his *I Love Lucy* co-star,
Vivian Vance
William Frawley, 1887–1966
actor

A mistress should be like a little country retreat near the town, not to dwell in constantly, but only for a night and away.

> *The Country Wife*
> **William Wycherly,** 1640–1716
> dramatist

You know you're getting old when you confide in your best friend that you are having an affair, and he says, "That's wonderful. Who's catering it?"

> **William Warfield,** 1920–2002
> baritone

So sweetly she bade me adieu, I thought that she bade me return.

> "Absence"
> **William Shenstone,** 1714–1763
> poet

Her mouth is a honey-blossom,
No doubt as the poet sings;
But within her lips, the petals,
Lurks a cruel bee that stings.

"The Sarcastic Fair"
William Dean Howells, 1837–1920
writer

In every heart there is a room
A sanctuary safe and strong
To heal the wounds from lovers past
Until a new one comes along

"And So It Goes"
Billy Joel, 1949–
musician/songwriter

A wail in the wind is all I hear;
A voice of woe for a lover's loss.

> "Tears in Spring"
> **William Ellery Channing,**
> 1817–1901
> poet

You can't sing about love unless you know about it.

> **Billy Eckstine,** 1914–1993
> singer

When my baby left me, she left me broken down
She said Goodbye Big Bill, I will see you in another town.

> "Big Bill Blues"
> **"Big Bill" Broonzy,** 1898–1958
> musician/songwriter

Ninety-nine percent of the world's lovers are not with their first choice. That's what makes the jukebox play.

Willie Nelson, 1933–
singer/songwriter

It doesn't bother me. I was also my wife's second choice, and we've been married twenty-five years.

as the second man offered a
coaching job
Billy Tubbs, 1935–
basketball coach

Courtship to marriage is as a very witty prologue to a very dull play.

The Old Bachelor
William Congreve, 1670–1729
dramatist

Love rarely overtakes; it mostly comes to meet us.

Wilhelm Stekel, 1868–1940
psychologist

The heart of marriage is memories; and if the two of you happen to have the same ones and can savor your reruns, then your marriage is a gift from the gods.

Bill Cosby, 1937–
actor/writer/producer

She lov'd me for the dangers I had pass'd,
And I lov'd her that she did pity them.

Othello
William Shakespeare, 1564–1616
dramatist/poet

Marriage is a wonderful invention: then again, so is a bicycle repair kit.

Billy Connolly, 1942–
comedian/actor

It is kisstomary to cuss the bride.

William Archibald Spooner,
1844–1930
Oxford don

I've been married five times, and people think that's some bizarre thing, yet I've got buddies who refuse to get married and have sex with fifteen people a week. I'm like, "Which is better?" At least I was trying.

Billy Bob Thornton, 1955–
actor/writer

Three of my wives were very good housekeepers. After we got divorced, they kept the house.

Willie Pep, 1922–2006
boxer

With all her experience, every woman expects to do better when she marries a second time, and some do.

William Feather, 1889–1981
publisher/writer

I think every woman is entitled to a middle husband she can forget.

Billy Sunday, 1862–1935
baseball player/evangelist

I have certainly known more men destroyed by the desire to have a wife and child and to keep them in comfort than I have seen destroyed by drink and harlots.

William Butler Yeats, 1865–1939
poet/dramatist

Love lasteth as long as the money endureth.

William Caxton, ca. 1422–1491
printer/bookseller

Love is only a dirty trick played on us to achieve the continuation of the species.

W. Somerset Maugham,
1874–1965
writer/dramatist

Yes, my soul says flesh should be a ladder up which soul climbs, wrong by wrong.

A Cry of Players
William Gibson, 1914–
dramatist

Lust will make a fool of any man, but it is only love that can truly ruin him.

Fatal Flaw
William Lashner, 1956–
writer/lawyer

Don't go to bed with anyone crazier than yourself.

William "Bill" Rotsler, 1926–1997
writer

The only time that most women give their orating husbands undivided attention is when the old boys mumble in their sleep.

Wilson Mizner, 1876–1933
dramatist/restaurateur

And a long tall woman will make a preacher lay his Bible down
But a big, fat mama will make a mule kick his stall down.

"Singin' the Blues"
Willie Jackson,
singer

She can kill with a smile,
She can wound with her eyes.

"She's Always a Woman"
Billy Joel, 1949–
musician/songwriter

Perhaps they were right in putting love into books. Perhaps it could not live anywhere else.

> *Light in August*
> **William Faulkner,** 1897–1962
> writer

The best sex education for kids is when Daddy pats Mommy on the fanny when he comes home from work.

> **William H. Masters,** 1915–2001
> physician/sexuality researcher

Natural man has only two primal passions: to get and to beget.

> **Sir William Osler,** 1849–1919
> physician

The proper time to influence the character of a child is about a hundred years before he is born.

William Ralph Inge, 1860–1954
priest/writer/educator

It is a wise father that knows his own child.

The Merchant of Venice
William Shakespeare, 1564–1616
dramatist/poet

A man never sees all that his mother has been to him until it's too late to let her know he sees it.

William Dean Howells, 1837–1920
writer

Even though your kids will consistently do the exact opposite of what you're telling them to do, you have to keep loving them just as much.

Bill Cosby, 1937–
actor/writer/producer

Wish to be an emperor, father, to begin with; then you can't be henpecked.

The Monkey's Paw
William Wymark Jacobs,
1863–1943
writer

Your parents are the best friends you have.

Hopalong Cassidy's Creed for American Boys and Girls
William Boyd, 1895–1972
actor

O dearest, dearest boy! My heart
For better lore would seldom yearn,
Could I but teach the hundredth part
Of what from thee I learn.

"An Anecdote for Fathers"
William Wordsworth, 1770–1850
poet

I never got along with my dad. Kids used to come up to me and say, "My dad can beat up your dad." I'd say, "Yeah? When?"

Bill Hicks, 1961–1994
comedian

The sign of a true friendship is when you can forgive success.

Guillermo del Toro, 1964–
filmmaker

It was June, I was fifteen, the weather was fine—so I stowed away. My mother cried and my father laughed and said, "Don't come back!"

on leaving Florida on a freighter
bound for New York
Billy Daniels, 1915–1988
singer

If a man's character is to be abused, say what you will, there's nobody like a relation to do the business.

Vanity Fair
William Makepeace Thackeray,
1811–1863
writer

A true friend knows your weaknesses but shows you your strengths; feels your fears but fortifies your faith; sees your anxieties but frees your spirit; recognizes your disabilities but emphasizes your possibilities.

William Arthur Ward, 1921–1994
writer

There can be no friendship where there is no freedom. Friendship loves a free air, and will not be fenced up in straight and narrow enclosures.

William Penn, 1644–1718
founder of Pennsylvania colony

Friends, books, a cheerful heart, and conscience clear are the most choice companions we have here.

William Mather, 1804–1859
geologist/cartographer

You can employ men and hire hands to work for you, but you must win their hearts to have them work with you.

William J. H. Boetcker, 1873–1962
minister

Though familiarity may not breed contempt, it takes off the edge of admiration.

William Hazlitt, 1778–1830
essayist/critic

You shall perceive how you
Mistake my fortunes; I am wealthy in my friends.

Timon of Athens
William Shakespeare, 1564–1616
dramatist/poet

How rare and wonderful is that flash of a moment when we realize we have discovered a friend.

William "Bill" Rotsler, 1926–1997
writer

Think where man's glory most begins and ends
And say my glory was I had such friends.

"The Municipal Gallery Revisited"
William Butler Yeats, 1865–1939
poet/dramatist

To the world you may be one person, but to one person you may be the world.

**William Griffith
("Bill W") Wilson,** 1895–1971
cofounder, Alcoholics Anonymous

Lean on me, when you're not strong
And I'll be your friend
I'll help you carry on
For it won't be long
'Til I'm gonna need
Somebody to lean on

"Lean On Me"
Bill Withers, 1938–
singer/songwriter

Friendship flourishes at the fountain of forgiveness.

William Arthur Ward, 1921–1994
writer

There is nothing final between friends.

William Jennings Bryan,
1860–1925
lawyer/U.S. congressman, Nebraska/
U.S. secretary of state

The man that hails you Tom or Jack,
And proves, by thumping on your back,
His sense of your great merit,
Is such a friend that one had need
Be very much his friend indeed
To pardon or to bear it.

"On Friendship"
William Cowper, 1731–1800
poet

He Started Out as a Child

It began something like this: "My mother did not put all her eggs in one basket, so to speak: she gave me a younger brother named Russell, who taught me what was meant by 'survival of the fittest.'" Since then Bill Cosby has given the world a comic tour of a man's life from boyhood, through marriage, to fatherhood and beyond.

As Dr. Cliff Huxtable, he was the patriarch of his own creation, *The Cosby Show*. The astute mix of real family values, genuine humor, and great casting provided American television viewers with a new kind of situation comedy—running eight seasons and scoring as the top-rated program for five consecutive years.

The sensibility came right out of his stand-up act: "I guess the real reason that my wife and I had children is the same reason that Napoleon had for invading Russia: it seemed like a good idea at the time."

Everybody's favorite Dad-of-the-Year has had his personal crises and sadness—and sorted through them under the public eye. Yet he remains the guy you believe truly means it when he says, "Fatherhood is pretending the present you love most is soap-on-a-rope."

two

Working Man

He is a wise man who wastes no energy on pursuits for which he is not fitted; and he is wiser still who, from among the things he can do well, chooses and resolutely follows the best.

William Ewart Gladstone,
1809–1898
British prime minister/chancellor
of the exchequer/member of
Parliament

I look at ordinary people in their suits, them with no scars, and I'm different. I don't fit with them. I'm where everybody's got scar tissue on their eyes and got noses like saddles. I go to conventions of old fighters like me and I see the scar tissue and all them flat noses and it's beautiful. Galento, may he rest in peace. Giardello, LaMotta, Carmen Basilio. What a sweetheart Basilio is! They talk like me, like they got rocks in their throats. Beautiful!

Willie Pastrano, 1935–1997
boxer

To business that we love we rise betime,
And go to 't with delight.

Antony and Cleopatra
William Shakespeare, 1564–1616
dramatist/poet

The abilities of a man must fall short on one side or the other, like too scanty a blanket when you are abed.

Sir William Temple, 1628–1699
statesman/essayist

A catcher must want to catch. He must make up his mind that it isn't the terrible job it is painted, and that he isn't going to say almost every day, "Why, oh why, with so many other positions in baseball, did I take up this one?"

Bill Dickey, 1907–1993
baseball player/manager

Poetry has never brought me in enough money to buy shoestrings.

William Wordsworth, 1770–1850
poet

In the simplest terms, it's a pleasure to borrow someone else's body and someone else's life. That's the craft, and it's a bit like voodoo, because you don't know exactly how you do it.

Willem Dafoe, 1955–
actor

An audience is never wrong. An individual member of it may be an imbecile, but a thousand imbeciles together in the dark—that is critical genius.

Billy Wilder, 1906–2002
filmmaker

Theater is, of course, a reflection of life. Maybe we have to improve life before we can hope to improve theater.

William Inge, 1913–1973
dramatist/writer

Since man is mortal, the only immortality possible for him is to leave something behind him that is immortal since it will always move. This is the artist's way of scribbling "Kilroy was here" on the wall of the final and irrevocable oblivion through which he must someday pass.

William Faulkner, 1897–1962
writer

You can't make a Hamlet without breaking a few egos.

William Goldman, 1931–
dramatist/screenwriter

If Richard Burton got sick the night before playing *Macbeth* in New York, he wouldn't be worried if Pee-Wee Herman replaced him for a day.

on replacement players during
football strike
Billy Ray Smith, 1961–
football player/sportscaster

The horse never knows I'm there until he needs me.

Willie Shoemaker, 1931–2003
jockey

The whole duty of a writer is to please and satisfy himself, and the true writer always plays to an audience of one.

William Strunk, 1869–1946
educator

The good writing of any age has always been the product of someone's neurosis, and we'd have mighty dull literature if all the writers that came along were a bunch of happy chuckleheads.

William Styron, 1925–2006
writer

To me, being a writer is like being an athlete. You can't pause to analyze the game while you're in it.

William Trevor, 1928–
writer

Nobody ever said, "Work ball!" They say, "Play ball!" To me, that means having fun.

Willie Stargell, 1940–2001
baseball player

Baseball is too much a sport to be a business and too much a business to be a sport.

William Wrigley, Jr., 1861–1932
businessman

A good hitting instructor is able to mold his teaching to the individual. If a guy stands on his head, you perfect that.

Bill Robinson, 1943–2007
baseball player

Trust is a must or your game is a bust.

> **Billy Welu,** 1932–1974
> bowler/broadcaster

Baseball is a game, yes. It is also a business. But what it is most truly is disguised combat. For all its gentility, its almost leisurely pace, baseball is violence under wraps.

> **Willie Mays, Jr.,** 1931–
> baseball player

If someone says, "Hey, I ran 100 miles this week. How far did you run?" ignore him! What the hell difference does it make? . . . The magic is in the man, not the 100 miles.

> **Bill Bowerman,** 1911–1999
> track coach

Golf puts a man's character on the anvil and his richest qualities—patience, poise, restraint—to the flame.

Billy Casper, 1931–
golfer

Some people think football is a matter of life and death. I can assure you it is much more serious than that.

Bill Shankly, 1913–1981
soccer manager

Baseball must be a great game to survive the fools who run it.

Bill Terry, 1898–1989
baseball player/manager

I'm a one-year manager only if the front office interferes with my running the club. If it leaves me alone, I'm a twenty-year manager.

Billy Martin, 1928–1989
baseball player/manager

You're either building something that's special or you have something that's special. In between is just no man's land.

Billy Beane, 1962–
baseball general manager

The best fighters I have known have all had that—the ability to keep the fight moving at their distance and always directly in front of them, pursuing their aim with a quiet purpose with all kinds of hell breaking loose on all sides from the throats of amateurs.

Bill Heinz, 1915–2008
sportswriter

The modern editor of a paper does not want facts. The editor wants novelty. He would prefer a novelty that is not a fact to a fact that is not a novelty.

William Randolph Hearst,
1863–1951
publisher/U.S. congressman,
New York

News work is highly addictive. It is the cocaine of crafts.

William F. Kerby, 1908–1989
publisher

The most successful column is the one that causes the reader to throw down the paper in a peak of fit.

William Safire, 1929–
writer

Knowing that I can't be around to see if my stuff lasts has given me such a huge sense of relief. No lobbying or politicking for my own work will make it any more or less irresistible.

William Bolcom, 1938–
composer/musician

Sounds like the blues are composed of feeling, finesse, and fear.

Billy Gibbons, 1949–
songwriter/musician

What I am saying to all you songwriters is to get yourself a good lawyer before you sign anything, no matter how much the company says they love you.

Willie Nelson, 1933–
singer/songwriter

I've never met a litigator who didn't think he was winning—right up until the moment the guillotine dropped.

William F. Baxter, 1929–1998
educator/U.S. assistant attorney
general

If all the world's economists were laid end to end, we wouldn't reach a conclusion.

William J. Baumol, 1922–
economist

I can play hardball as well as anybody. That's what I did, cut people's hearts out. On the other hand, I do it to cure them, to heal them, to make them better.

Bill Frist, 1952–
physician/U.S. senator, Tennessee

One of the first duties of the physician is to educate the masses not to take medicine.

Sir William Osler, 1849–1919
physician

I can only think of one experience that might exceed in interest a few hours spent under water and that would be a journey to Mars.

Charles William "Will" Beebe,
1877–1962
naturalist/explorer

Physicists use the wave theory on Mondays, Wednesdays and Fridays and the particle theory on Tuesdays, Thursdays and Saturdays.

Sir William Henry Bragg,
1862–1942
physicist/chemist

For me, the creative process, first of all, requires a good nine hours of sleep a night.

William N. Lipscomb, Jr., 1919–
chemist

I get satisfaction of three kinds. One is creating something, one is being paid for it and one is the feeling that I haven't just been sitting on my ass all afternoon.

William F. Buckley, Jr., 1925–2008
writer/political commentator

The sons of Johann Sebastian Bach thought that Papa was pretty good, but they would show how to really write music. They were really very good, but two centuries later you hardly know of them, but you still know of Papa. Just because it's new, doesn't make it better.

Bill Gottlieb, 1917–2006
journalist/photographer

Creativity is an area in which younger people have a tremendous advantage, since they have an endearing habit of always questioning past wisdom and authority. They say to themselves that there must be a better way. Ninety-nine times out of a hundred, they discover that the existing, traditional way is the best. But it is that one percent that counts.

William R. Hewlett, 1913–2001
engineer/businessman

All the world is competent to judge my pictures except those who are of my profession.

William Hogarth, 1697–1764
artist/satirist

With the arrogance of youth, I determined to do no less than to transform the world with Beauty.

William Morris, 1834–1896
writer/designer

Artists are, above all, men who want to become inhuman.

Guillaume Apollinaire, 1880–1918
writer/art critic

All the great craving desires of humanity have been promised and attained through the message of art.

William Stanley Braithwaite,
1878–1962
writer

It is the function of the artist to evoke the experience of surprised recognition: to show the viewer what he knows but does not know that he knows.

William S. Burroughs, 1914–1997
writer

The writer is a spiritual anarchist, as in the depth of his soul every man is. He is discontented with everything and everybody. The writer is everybody's best friend and only true enemy—the good and great enemy.

William Saroyan, 1908–1981
writer

I always urge people to write in the first person. . . . Writing is an act of ego and you might as well admit it.

William Zinsser, 1922–
writer/educator

A writer lives, at best, in a state of astonishment.

William Sansom, 1912–1976
writer

Every filmmaker, every journalist has to be arrogant. You have to say "I have the truth, you got to pay attention, you got to listen."

Bill Moyers, 1934–
broadcast journalist

Never let truth get in the way of a good story.

William H. Macy, 1950–
actor

Sometimes I get a little sad because I look out into that audience and I know it's not going to be there for very long, that the moment is going to be gone.

Billy Corgan, 1967–
musician/songwriter

The performer who takes the stage must believe that he is fascinating.

> **Bill T. Jones,** 1952–
> dancer/choreographer

Jazz is like pure mountain air that regenerates the soul of man.

> **Billy Taylor,** 1921–
> musician/composer/educator

The great artist gets right to the heart of the matter.

> **Bill Evans,** 1929–1980
> musician/composer

For the mystic what is how. For the craftsman how is what. For the artist what and how are one.

> **William McElcheran,** 1927–1999
> artist

I flatter myself that I feel more than I express on canvas; but I know that is not so.

> **William Morris Hunt,** 1824–1879
> artist

Art without control is like a living man without a head—it walks but it doesn't talk.

> **Bill Russo,** 1928–2003
> musician/composer

After God created the world, He made man and woman. Then, to keep the whole thing from collapsing, He invented humor.

> **Guillermo Mordillo,** 1932–
> cartoonist

I always said we had a lot in common: we both did a feature about kids and family values. He had five children; I had five children. He was born in 1922; I was born in 1922. He made a million dollars a week; I was born in 1922.

> *Family Circus* creator, on *Peanuts* creator Charles Schulz
> **Bil Keane,** 1922–
> cartoonist

Analyzing humour is like dissecting a frog. Few people are interested and the frog dies of it.

W. C. Fields, 1880–1946
actor/comedian

I have only been funny about seventy-four percent of the time. Yes, I think that is right. Seventy-four percent of the time.

Will Ferrell, 1967–
actor/writer

There are four of us who've tried show business. Five if you insist on counting my sister the nun, who does liturgical dance.

about his family
Bill Murray, 1950–
actor

The camera is a weapon against the tragedy of things, against their disappearing.

> **Ernst Wilhelm "Wim" Wenders,**
> 1945–
> filmmaker

Violence is not funny.

> **William Friedkin,** 1935–
> filmmaker

It is as the breath of life to me . . . the rush of the wind that cuts your face, the pounding hooves of the pursuing posse, and then the clouds of dust! Through the cloud of dust comes the faint voice of the director, "Now, Bill, OK! Glad you made it! Great stuff, Bill, great stuff!"

> **William S. Hart,** 1864–1946
> actor

It's eighty percent script and twenty percent you get great actors. There's nothing else to it.

William Wyler, 1902–1981
filmmaker

Acting is playing—it's actually going out on a playground with the other kids and being in the game, and I need that.

Billy Bob Thornton, 1955–
actor/writer

Some of the greatest love affairs I've known have involved one actor—unassisted.

Wilson Mizner, 1876–1933
dramatist/restaurateur

When designing an actor's home, if I can give him plenty of mirrors quietly and never mention it, it is a happy solution.

William "Billy" Haines,
1900–1973
actor/decorator

Art is not a special sauce applied to ordinary cooking; it is the cooking itself if it is good.

William Richard Lethaby,
1857–1931
architect/historian

No old stuff for me! No bestial copyings of arches and columns and cornices! Me, I'm new! Avanti!

William Van Allen, 1883–1954
architect

No man who owns his own house and lot can be a communist. He has too much to do.

William J. Levitt, 1907–1994
real estate developer

The truth isn't the truth until people believe you, and they can't believe you if they don't know what you're saying, and they can't know what you're saying if they don't listen to you, and they won't listen to you if you're not interesting, and you won't be interesting unless you say things imaginatively, originally, freshly.

Bill Bernbach, 1911–1982
advertising executive

People's imagination is what brings the terror to reading a book.

William Peter Blatty, 1928–
writer/filmmaker

I want to hold one word through a whole line of melody, to linger with it all the way down. I didn't want to let go of that no more than I wanted to let go of the woman I loved. I didn't want to lose it.

William Orville "Lefty" Frizzell,
1928–1975
singer/songwriter

I sat down one night and wrote the line rock, rock, rock everybody. I was going to use the word "stomp"—like rock, rock, rock and then stomp, stomp, stomp. But that didn't fit. I went from one word to another and finally came up with "roll."

Bill Haley, 1925–1981
singer/songwriter

If you play a tune and a person don't tap their feet, don't play the tune.

William James "Count" Basie,
1904–1984
musician/composer

If I'm in Vegas tomorrow, and on the corner the next day, I'm still the same person . . . I want to reach everybody with my music.

Billy Paul, 1934–
singer

As long as they can wheel me up to the piano, with the help of the good Lord, I'll play . . .

Willie "The Lion" Smith,
1897–1973
musician

It's Scotch bagpipes and ole-time fiddlin'. It's Methodist and Holiness and Baptist. It's blues and jazz, and it has a high lonesome sound. It's plain music that tells a good story. It's played from my heart to your heart, and it will touch you. Bluegrass is music that matters.

Bill Monroe, 1911–1996
musician

When I see a book that's supposed to be "gut-crunching suspense," I always ask myself, "do I sincerely want my guts crunched this week?"

William L. DeAndrea, 1952–1996
writer

Who writes poetry imbibes honey from the poisoned lips of life.

William Rose Benét, 1886–1950
editor/writer

A song is like a newspaper. It's capable of carrying a number of different messages. Some of them are advertisers, some of them are editorial, some of them are reportage, some of them are sport.

Billy Bragg, 1957–
musician/songwriter

Closing the book, I find I have left my head inside. It is dark in here, but the chapters open their beautiful spaces and give a rustling sound . . .

"An Afternoon in the Stacks"
William Stafford, 1914–1993
poet

One's complete sentences are attempts, as often as not, to complete an incomplete self with words.

William H. Gass, 1924–
writer

Do you want adjectives or information?

> to editor who asked him to "beef up"
> a story
> **Will McDonough,** 1935–2003
> sportswriter

You fly off to a strange land, eagerly abandoning all the comforts of home, and then expend vast quantities of time and money in a largely futile attempt to recapture the comforts that you wouldn't have lost if you hadn't left home in the first place.

> **Bill Bryson,** 1951–
> travel writer

Poetry is my cheap means of transportation. By the end of the poem the reader should be in a different place from where he started. I would like him to be slightly disoriented at the end, like I drove him outside of town at night and dropped him off in a cornfield.

Billy Collins, 1941–
poet

A Bill by Any Other Name

Something there is about a man named William—when he isn't stuck with a nickname, he makes one up, shortens his seven letters by one or two (or even three), or throws it all aside for a monogram.

William Christopher Handy and William Claude Fields settled on W. C., the abbreviation's British connotation aside. Puppeteer Bil Baird said nobody ever pronounced the second "l" anyway. William Abbott was Bud when he explained "who's on first" to Lou Costello.

Wilson Mizner was a Bill. Willie was what friends and family called W. (William) Somerset Maugham. Jack Dempsey struck a blow against his Williamhood, but philosopher Georg Wilhelm Friedrich Hegel was called Wilhelm at home. (Perhaps occasionally "Thoughtful Willy"?)

The descriptive can be helpful, or can get out of hand. *Slick Willie* applied to Sutton before Clinton. The music world has a "Blind Willie" Johnson and a "Blind Willie" McTell—plus "Little Willie" John and "Little Willie" Jackson. "Fast Willie" Parker plays football; "Fast Willie" Jackson was styled as a comic book soul-cousin to Archie Andrews.

Big Bill could be a tennis great, a pitcher, a labor leader, or possibly half the membership of the musician's union. William Hazlitt wrote that "A nickname is the heaviest stone that the devil can throw at a man." But maybe it takes a very big Bill indeed to resist the temptation.

three

Noble and Notorious

It matters not how strait the gate,
How charged with punishments the scroll,
I am the master of my fate;
I am the captain of my soul.

"Invictus"
William Ernest Henley, 1849–1903
poet

Act as if what you do makes a difference. It does.

William James, 1842–1910
psychologist/philosopher

Every human being is intended to have a character of his own; to be what no other is, and to do what no other can do.

William Ellery Channing,
1780–1842
theologian

I weigh the man, not his title; 'tis not the king's stamp can make the metal better or heavier.

The Plain Dealer
William Wycherley, 1640–1716
dramatist

Nothing spoils fun like finding out it builds character.

Calvin and Hobbes
Bill Watterson, 1958–
cartoonist

Your reputation is what people say about you. Your character is what God and your wife know about you.

Billy Sunday, 1862–1935
baseball player/evangelist

Your father believed in one thing. I believe in another. You believe in something else. But it doesn't matter a tuppenny damn what one believes in, so long as it's worth believing in. It's faith, sonny, that does it. Faith and purpose.

The Fortunate Youth
William John Locke, 1863–1930
writer

If honor be your clothing, the suit will last a lifetime; but if clothing be your honor, it will soon be worn threadbare.

William Arnot, 1808–1875
clergyman

Oh, lot o' times I sit and t'ink
How nice, 'twould be, gee whiz!
If a feller was de feller
Dat his mudder t'inks he is.

"If I Only Was the Fellow"
Will S. Adkin
writer

This is the final test of a gentleman: his respect for those who can be of no possible value to him.

William Lyon Phelps,
1865–1943
writer/educator

People are always making rules for themselves and always finding loop-holes.

William "Bill" Rotsler, 1926–1997
writer

Our desires attract supporting reasons as a magnet the iron filings.

William Macneile Dixon,
1866–1946
poet/educator

No tendency is quite so strong in human nature as the desire to lay down rules of conduct for other people.

William Howard Taft, 1857–1930
U.S. president/U.S. Supreme Court
chief justice

You can't learn too soon that the most useful thing about a principle is that it can always be sacrificed to expediency.

W. Somerset Maugham, 1874–1965
writer/dramatist

In a competitive market, compromise—that is, accepting half a loaf—is often essential for survival. But compromise of a basic belief, such as truth or seeking to do what is right, does not result in half a loaf. It ends up being half a baby. . . . Half a baby is no baby at all. Half a belief is no belief at all.

C. William Pollard, 1938–
businessman

A principle is not a principle until it costs you something.

Bill Bernbach, 1911–1982
advertising executive

If we are but sure the end is right, we are too apt to gallop over all bounds to compass it; not considering the lawful ends may be very unlawfully attained.

William Penn, 1644–1718
founder of Pennsylvania colony

The circumstances of the world are so variable that an irrevocable purpose or opinion is almost synonymous with a foolish one.

William Henry Seward, 1801–1872
governor/U.S. senator, New York/U.S.
secretary of state

It often takes more courage to change one's opinion than to keep it.

Willy Brandt, 1913–1992
West German chancellor

Zealous men are ever displaying to you the strength of their belief, while judicious men are showing you the grounds of it.

William Shenstone, 1714–1763
poet

As the essence of courage is to stake one's life on a possibility, so the essence of faith is to believe that the possibility exists.

William Salter, 1821–1910
minister

To try may be to die, but not to care is never to be born.

William Redfield, 1927–1976
actor

Men never cling to their dreams with such tenacity as at the moment when they are losing faith in them, and know it, but do not dare yet to confess it to themselves.

William Graham Sumner,
1840–1910
educator

A man who hides behind the hypocrite is smaller than the hypocrite.

William Edward Biederwolf,
1867–1939
evangelist/writer

There smites nothing so sharp, nor smelleth so sour as shame.

Piers Plowman
William Langland, ca. 1332–1400
poet

Prisons are built with stones of Law, brothels with bricks of Religion.

The Marriage of Heaven and Hell
William Blake, 1757–1827
artist/poet

A burglar who respects his art always takes his time before taking anything else.

William Sidney Porter (O. Henry),
1862–1910
writer

Stop them damn pictures. I don't care so much what the papers write about me. My constituents can't read. But, damn it, they can see pictures.

on cartoon images of himself
William Marcy "Boss" Tweed,
1823–1878
politician

I've always loved movies about con men. I think con men are as American as apple pie.

Bill Paxton, 1955–
actor

It's better to tell the truth and run, than to lie and get caught in the act.

William Crosbie Hunter, 1866–?
writer

I came here to die, not to make a speech.

when asked at his hanging for any last words
Crawford "Cherokee Bill" Goldsby, 1876-1896
Old West outlaw

The jury, passing on the prisoner's life,
May in the sworn twelve have a thief or two
Guiltier than him they try.

Measure for Measure
William Shakespeare, 1564–1616
dramatist/poet

I do not like the man's face. He looks as if he will live to be hanged.

at age fourteen, declining an apprenticeship
William Blake, 1757–1827
artist/poet

So, from the body of one guilty deed,
A thousand ghostly fears, and haunting thoughts, proceed!

"Echo, upon the Gemmi"
William Wordsworth, 1770–1850
poet

If mob law is going to rule, better dismiss judge, sheriff, etc., and let all take chances alike.

William H. "Billy the Kid" Bonney,
1859–1881
Old West outlaw

A Smith and Wesson beats four aces.

> **"Canada Bill" Jones,** 18??–1880
> card sharp

Which is better—to have laws and agree, or to hunt and kill?

> *Lord of the Flies*
> **William Golding,** 1911–1993
> writer

I'm just one drink away from being an alcoholic and just one deal away from being back in prison.

> **Billie Sol Estes,** 1924–
> financier

As some day it may happen that a victim must be found,
I've got a little list—I've got a little list
Of society offenders who might well be under ground
And who never would be missed—who never would be
    missed!

The Mikado
Sir W. S. Gilbert, 1836–1911
lyricist/dramatist

We try to buy ourselves into good relationship with God. We
bow Him out of our lives in normal things and then think we
can ingratiate ourselves by a few religious exercises on Sunday.
The attitude seems to be: Lord, I'll do my part and you do
Yours, but let's not become too intimate in the process.

William Ward Ayer, 1892–1985
clergyman

In Los Angeles, it's like they jog for two hours a day and then they think they're morally right. That's when you want to choke people, you know?

Liam Neeson, 1952–
actor

Don't shoot me anymore, I'm killed.

to Buckskin Frank Leslie, at end of gunfight
Billy Claiborne, 1860–1882
Old West outlaw

You can get more with a kind word and a gun than you can get with just a kind word.

Willie Sutton, 1901–1980
bank robber

I am not over-fond of resisting temptation.

Vathek
William Beckford, 1760–1844
writer/politician

If one starts with the notion that anything a man does which gives him pleasure is probably sinful, it is only one step to think it is harmful and the next thing to do is to pass a law against it.

William B. Ober, 1921–1993
physician

Amid all the definitions proposed for man the most truthful would in fact be that he is the religious animal.

William E. Barrett, 1913–1992
philosopher

Where there is no free agency, there can be no morality. Where there is no temptation, there can be little claim to virtue. Where the routine is rigorously prescribed by law, the law, and not the man, must have the credit of the conduct.

William Hickling Prescott,
1796–1859
historian

'Tis not the dying for a faith that's so hard, Master Harry— every man of every nation has done that—'tis the living up to it that is difficult, as I know to my cost.

The History of Henry Esmond esq.
William Makepeace Thackeray,
1811–1863
writer

We must alter our lives in order to alter our hearts, for it is impossible to live one way and pray another.

William Law, 1686–1761

clergyman

Those who know me as a church usher can't believe that when I retired from the NHL in 1966 after 20 years of service, I was the league's all-time penalty minute leader.

Bill Gadsby, 1927–

hockey player

There is no wild beast so ferocious as Christians who differ concerning their faith.

William Edward Hartpole Lecky,

1838–1903

historian/poet

Some can only eat out of the silent dish, but I can not only eat out of that one, but out of the shouting dish, and jumping dish, and every other dish. My comrades used to tell me that was no religion, dancing, shouting, and making so much to-do, but I was born in the fire and could not live in the smoke.

> **Billy "God's Man with a Shout" Bray,** 1794–1868
> preacher

Some persons think that they have to look like a hedgehog to be pious.

> **Billy Sunday,** 1862–1935
> baseball player/evangelist

To do evil so that good may come of it is for bunglers in politics as well as morals.

> **William Penn,** 1644–1718
> founder of Pennsylvania colony

It's hard to be religious when certain people are never incinerated by bolts of lightning.

Calvin and Hobbes
Bill Watterson, 1958–
cartoonist

God is infinitely bigger than any problem you ever had or will have, and every time you call a problem unsolvable, you mock God.

Bill Hybels, 1952–
minister

I do not feel obliged to believe that the same God who has endowed us with sense, reason, and intellect has intended us to forgo their use.

William Falconer, 1732–1769
poet/sailor

The most perplexing form of evil, and especially so for all idealists, is that kind of evil which comes out of our efforts to do good. Perhaps when we try to do good without love, we create evil.

William Irwin Thompson, 1938–
philosopher/poet

Dear Mother, dear Mother, the Church is cold,
But the Ale-house is healthy & pleasant & warm . . .
But if at the Church they would give us some ale,
And a pleasant fire our souls to regale,
We'd sing and we'd pray all the live-long day,
And never once wish from the Church to stray.

"The Little Vagabond"
William Blake, 1757–1827
artist/poet

To be engaged in opposing wrong affords, under the conditions of our mental constitution, but a slender guarantee for being right.

William Ewart Gladstone,
1809–1898
British prime minister/chancellor of
the exchequer/member of Parliament

The greatest form of praise is the sound of consecrated feet seeking out the lost and helpless.

Billy Graham, 1918–
evangelist

The undevout astronomer must be mad.

Sir William Herschel,
1738–1822
astronomer/composer

All great and honorable actions are accompanied with great difficulties.

William Bradford, 1590–1657
governor, Plymouth colony,
Massachusetts

I asked Mother Earth for strength, that I might have my
    way,
I was given weakness, that I might feel the need for Her.
I asked to live happily, that I might enjoy life,
I was given life, that I might live happily,
I received nothing I asked for, yet all my wishes came true.

Billy Mills, 1938–
athlete

The most curious anomaly among the race of man, the red man of America, is passing away beneath our eyes into the infinite solitude. The possession of the same noble qualities which we affect to reverence among our nation makes us kill him . . . if he would be our slave he might live, but as he won't be that, won't toil and delve and hew for us, and will persist in hunting, fishing, and roaming over the beautiful prairie land which the Great Spirit gave him; in a word, since he will be free—we kill him.

Sir William Francis Butler,
1838–1910
British general/writer

The pious ones of Plymouth, who, reaching the Rock, first fell upon their own knees and then upon the aborigines.

William Maxwell Evarts,
1818–1901
U.S. secretary of state/attorney general/senator, New York

While you ask yourselves, "what do they, the Indians, want?," you have only to look at the unjust laws made for them, and say they want what I want, which is that "all men must operate under one general law."

William Apess, 1798–1839
writer/minister

If it be an evil to judge rashly or untruly any single man, how much a greater sin it is to condemn a whole people.

William Penn, 1644–1718
founder of Pennsylvania colony

One ever feels his twoness—an American, a Negro; two souls, two thoughts, two unreconciled strivings; two warring ideals in one dark body, whose dogged strength alone keeps it from being torn asunder.

W. E. B. DuBois, 1868–1963
educator/writer/historian

. . . **I** swear, while life-blood warms my throbbing veins,
Still to oppose and thwart, with heart and hand,
Thy brutalizing sway—till Afric's chains
Are burst, and Freedom rules the rescued land,
Trampling Oppression and his iron rod:
Such is the vow I take—SO HELP ME GOD!

> **William Lloyd Garrison,** 1805–
> 1879
> abolitionist/journalist

Some things you must always be unable to bear. Some things you must never stop refusing to bear. Injustice and outrage and dishonor and shame. No matter how young you are or how old you have got. Not for kudos and not for cash. Your picture in the paper nor money in the bank, neither. Just refuse to bear them.

> *Intruder in the Dust*
> **William Faulkner,** 1897–1962
> writer

If mankind had wished for what is right, they might have had it long ago.

William Hazlitt, 1778–1830
essayist/critic

Could it be that the road to technology represents a rush to destruction, and that the road to spirituality represents the slower path that the traditional native people have traveled and are now seeking again? The earth is not scorched on this trail. The grass is still growing there.

William Commanda, 1913–
Algonquin tribal elder

There are two eyes in the human head—the eye of mystery, and the eye of harsh truth—the hidden and the open.

Bill Holm, 1925–
art historian

Too many of our prejudices are like pyramids upside down. They rest on tiny, trivial incidents, but they spread upward and outward until they fill our minds.

William McChesney Martin, Jr.,
1906–1998
U.S. federal reserve chairman

It's eider dis or dat wid me. Dere ain't no in-between.

Bill Guthrie, 1886–1950
baseball umpire

One leg by truth supported, one by lies,
They sidle to the goal with awkward pace,
Secure of nothing—but to lose the race.

"The Progress of Error"
William Cowper, 1731–1800
poet

A liar begins with making falsehood appear like truth, and ends with making truth itself appear like falsehood.

William Shenstone, 1714–1763
poet

But stand back now; the truth, clearly spoken, is always your best weapon. Calmly spoken, it can burn a hole through the hardest heart.

Bill Chickering, 1951–
writer

For fear in wrath you play the fool,
Take four-and-twenty hours to cool.

"Maxims"
William Hutton, 1723–1815
businessman/historian/poet

It is discouraging to try to be a good neighbor in a bad neighborhood.

William R. Castle, 1878–1963
diplomat

Expressing anger is a form of public littering.

Willard "Will" Gaylin, 1925–
psychiatrist/educator

That they may have a little peace, even the best dogs are compelled to snarl occasionally.

William Feather, 1889–1981
publisher/writer

Do not judge in anger, for, though the anger passes, the judgment remains!

William Q. Judge, 1851–1896
cofounder, the Theosophical Society

An angry player can't argue with the back of an umpire who is walking away.

Bill Klem, 1874–1951
baseball umpire

One should not lose one's temper unless one is certain of getting more and more angry to the end.

William Butler Yeats, 1865–1939
poet/dramatist

We must wake ourselves up! Or somebody else will take our place, and bear our cross, and thereby rob us of our crown.

William Booth, 1829–1912
minister/founder, the Salvation Army

But one thing's settled with me: To appreciate Heaven well, 'Tis good for a man to have some fifteen minutes of hell!

"Gone With a Handsomer Man"
Will Carleton, 1845–1912
poet

The road to ruin is in good repair; the travelers pay the expense of it.

Sir William Gurney Benham,
1859–1944
businessman/writer

Life has no smooth road for any of us; and in the bracing atmosphere of a high aim the very roughness stimulates the climber to steadier steps till the legend, "over steep ways to the stars," fulfills itself.

William Croswell Doane,
1832–1913
Episcopal bishop

There is never a better measure of what a person is than what he does when he's absolutely free to choose.

William M. Bulger, 1934–
politician/educator

Ambition hath one heel nailed in hell, though she stretch her fingers to touch the heavens.

William Lilly, 1602–1681
astrologer

One motion—and the stream is crossed,
So dark, so deep!
And I shall triumph, or be lost
In endless sleep.

"The Rubicon"
William Winter, 1836–1917
critic

We think we can change everything and we can change nothing. Our very thoughts and motives and ideals are only bits of the Eternal Force that holds the stars balanced in the skies and keeps the earth for a moment solid to our feet. I cannot move it. I cannot affect it. I cannot shake it. It alone is.

William Lane, 1861–1917
journalist

A man may fight fiercely to hold his own in business; but he does not need to fight to get ahead of someone in the elevator, or up the car steps, or at the post office window.

William H. Hamby, 1876–1928
writer

Let no one suppose that evolution will ever exempt us from our struggles, "You forget," said the Devil, with a chuckle, "that I have been evolving, too."

William Ralph Inge, 1860–1954
priest/writer/educator

Wild, Wild Westerners

The American Old West had its share of bad guys, and, to keep them in line, its share of good guys. Among the forgotten, the legendary and the downright fictitious, a whole passel of 'em were Williams.

William Barclay "Bat" Masterson and Bill Tilghman were on the side of law and order. In the lawless and ornery camp were Dalton gang standout Bill Doolin and his colleagues "Little Bill" Raidler, William Blake, and Bill Powers. "Buffalo Bill" Brooks began as a lawman but then went bad—not the last to slip that way—but William "Port" Stockton converted the other direction, to keep things in balance.

"Buffalo Bill" Cody and "Pawnee Bill" Lillie each founded "Wild West" shows that toured the

United States and Europe. Crawford "Cherokee Bill" Goldsby, the son of a freed slave and a Cherokee mother, was considered one of the most dangerous outlaws in the Indian territories. Then there was the great Bill Pickett, also the son of a former slave and a Cherokee, remembered as one of the great cowboys of the nineteenth and twentieth centuries.

What did "Curly Bill" Brocius, "Russian Bill" Tattenbaum, and "Brazen Bill" Brazelton have in common with "Mormon Bill" Delaney, "Whiskey Bill" Graves, "Rattling Bill" Longley, "Flapjack Bill" Nicholson, Bill "The Missouri Kid" Rudolph, and "Colorado Bill" Wiley? All were either shot dead by lawmen, hanged by judges, or lynched by vigilantes. Bill "The Cherokee Kid" Cook and "Old Bill" Miner lived out their years in prison—a kind of justice that apparently seemed peskily time-consuming in the era.

One of the most infamous of the nicknamed was William H. Bonney. Or was he no William at all, but Henry McCarty? Whatever the legal name of this New York City–born legend, we remember him as Billy the Kid.

Then there was James Butler "Wild Bill" Hickok. A man with a ski-slope nose and protruding upper lip, he had been nicknamed "Duckbill," which he managed to shorten to Bill and then lengthen to the more fear-inspiring sobriquet. Hickok alternated law enforcement duties with gambling opportunities— and met his death at a poker table, supposedly holding the famed "Aces and Eights" or "dead man's hand." A century later Wild Bill was in the first class inducted into the Poker Hall of Fame.

four

Wit, Wisdom,
Wisecracks

I would like to take you seriously but to do so would affront your intelligence.

William F. Buckley, Jr.,
1925–2008
writer/political commentator

Tact is the interpreter of all riddles, the surmounter of all difficulties, the remover of all obstacles.

William Scargill, 1787–1836
minister/writer

Nothing is often a good thing to say, and always a clever thing to say.

> **Will Durant,** 1885–1981
> philosopher/historian

It was not my best hour. It was not even my best hour and a half.

> on his keynote address at the 1988
> Democratic convention
> **Bill Clinton,** 1946–
> U.S. president/governor, Arkansas

A good listener is not only popular everywhere, but after a while he knows something.

> **Wilson Mizner,** 1876–1933
> dramatist/restaurateur

Wit is the salt of conversation, not the food.

William Hazlitt, 1778–1830
essayist/critic

In America we pride ourselves on being able to get a pizza
to our door faster than an ambulance.

Will Durst, 1952–
political satirist

If I may kiss no mouth that's red,
Give me the open mouth instead
Of a black bottle of old wine
To gurgle in its neck and mine.

''To The New Year''
William Henry Davies, 1871–1940
poet/writer

They used to have a fish on the menu that was smoked, grilled, and peppered. They did everything to this fish but pistol-whip it and dress it in Bermuda shorts.

Bill Geist, 1945–
writer/commentator

Dessert is probably the most important stage of the meal, since it will be the last thing your guests remember before they pass out all over the table.

William Powell, 1892–1984
actor

Nature provides a free lunch, but only if we control our appetites.

William D. Ruckelshaus, 1932–
lawyer/U.S. Environmental Protection
Agency director

I've been asked if I ever get the DTs; I don't know; it's hard to tell where Hollywood ends and the DTs begin.

W. C. Fields, 1880–1946
actor/comedian

No little boy or girl should ever drink rum or whiskey, unless they want to become drunkards.

The First Eclectic Reader (1836)
William Holmes McGuffey,
1800–1873
educator

So let's sink another drink
'Cause it'll give me time to think.

"Dancing With Myself,"
with Tony James, 1958–
Billy Idol, 1955–
musician/songwriter

Love takes the taint of years,
And beauty disappears,
But wine in worth matures
The longer it endures.

"The Love in Her Eyes Lay Sleeping"
William Forster, 1818–1882
politician/poet

Many a man takes to beer, not from the love of beer, but from a natural craving for the light, warmth, company, and comfort which is thrown in along with the beer, and which he cannot get excepting by buying beer.

William Booth, 1829–1912
minister/founder, the Salvation Army

I love exercise. I could watch it all day.

Bill Russell, 1934–
basketball player/coach

I drink it as the Fates ordain it.
Come, fill it, and have done with rhymes;
Fill up the lonely glass, and drain it
In memory of dear old times.

"The Ballad of Bouillabaisse"
William Makepeace Thackeray,
1811–1863
writer

As a nation we are dedicated to keeping physically fit—and parking as close to the stadium as possible.

Bill Vaughan, 1915–1977
writer

I don't have an ulcer. I'm a carrier. I give them to other people.

Bill Fitch, 1934–
basketball coach

Anything other than death is a minor injury.

> **Bill Muncey,** 1928–1981
> hydroplane racer

I've got this dark little lump of cold grief or something over my heart. It could, of course, be wind.

> *Alfie*
> **Bill Naughton,** 1910–1992
> writer/dramatist

It's the same the whole world over,
It's the poor what gets the blame,
It's the rich what gets the pleasure,
Isn't it a blooming shame?

> "She Was Poor But She Was Honest"
> **Billy Bennett,** 1887–1942
> comedian

It was a Rolls Royce that hit me, that was some satisfaction. Think of my feelings if a Ford had fixed me up this way.

William Jerome, 1865–1932
songwriter

The name of my condition is cartilage hair hypoplasia, but you can just call me Billy.

Billy Barty, 1924–2000
actor

It is the manner of hypochondriacs to change often their physician . . . for a physician who does not admit the reality of the disease cannot be supposed to take much pains to cure it.

William Cullen, 1710–1790
physician/chemist

The trouble with being poor is that it takes up all your time.

Willem de Kooning, 1904–1997
artist

The mortgage market changes virtually from day to day, so you can wait a few weeks and, if you haven't committed suicide in the meantime, try again, even with the same lenders.

William G. Connolly
editor/writer

We was po' folks livin' in a rich folks world,
we sure was a hungry bunch.
If the wolf had ever come to our front door
he'd had to brought a picnic lunch.

"Po' Folks"
Bill Anderson, 1937–
singer/songwriter

When a man is in love or in debt, someone else has the advantage.

Bill Ballance, 1918–2004
broadcaster

Never invest your money in anything that eats or needs painting.

Billy Rose, 1899–1966
showman

I'd rather be a lamppost in Chicago than a millionaire in any other city.

William A. Hulbert, 1832–1882
businessman/baseball pioneer

When you are young and impecunious, society conditions you to exchange time for money, and this is quite as it should be. Very few people are hurt by having to work for a living. But as you become more affluent, it somehow is very, very difficult to reverse that process and begin trading money for time.

William H. Rehnquist, 1924–2005
U.S. Supreme Court justice/chief justice

If you bet a horse, that's gambling. If you bet you can make three spades, that's entertainment. If you bet cotton will go up three points, that's business. See the difference?

William Sherrod, 1835–1919
U.S. congressman, Alabama

In the bad old days, there were three easy ways of losing money—racing being the quickest, women the pleasantest, and farming the most certain.

William Pitt Amherst, 1773–1857
governor-general of India

Buy old masters. They fetch a better price than old mistresses.

William Maxwell Aitken, Lord Beaverbrook, 1879–1964
British member of Parliament/ publisher

Don't gamble; take all your savings and buy some good stock and hold it till it goes up, then sell it. If it don't go up, don't buy it.

Will Rogers, 1879–1935
humorist/actor

There are many in this old world of ours who hold that things break about even for all of us. I have observed, for example, that we all get about the same amount of ice. The rich get it in the summertime and the poor get it in winter.

William Barclay "Bat" Masterson, 1853–1921
U.S. marshal/journalist

When lying, be emphatic and indignant, thus behaving like your children.

William Feather, 1889–1981
publisher/writer

Even when I was little, I was big.

William "The Refrigerator" Perry, 1962–
football player

I'm like Daffy Duck in the cartoons. I'm black, I've got big feet, and I'm always bitching.

Billy Sample, 1955–
baseball player/commentator

I lost it in the sun.

on a missed ground ball
Billy Loes, 1929–
baseball player

In high school I took a little English, some science, some hubcaps and some wheel covers.

William James "Gates" Brown,
1939–
baseball player/coach

I pray that no child of mine would ever descend into such a place as a library. They are indeed most dangerous places and unfortunate is she or he who is lured into such a hellhole of enjoyment, stimulus, facts, passion and fun.

Willy Russell, 1947–
dramatist/composer

A college education is one of the few things a person is willing to pay for and not get.

William Lowe Bryan, 1860–1955
educator

If there is anything the nonconformist hates worse than a conformist, it's another nonconformist who doesn't conform to the prevailing standard of nonconformity.

Bill Vaughan, 1915–1977
writer

If your lips would keep from slips,
Five things observe with care;
To whom you speak, of whom you speak,
And how, and when, and where.

W. E. Norris, 1847–1925
writer

Since knowledge is but sorrow's spy,
It is not safe to know.

The Just Italian
William Davenant, 1606–1668
poet/dramatist

Wisdom is ofttimes nearer when we stoop
Than when we soar.

"The Excursion"
William Wordsworth, 1770–1850
poet

A fool must now and then be right by chance.

> "Conversation"
> **William Cowper,** 1731–1800
> poet

The greatest vested interest is not property but ignorance.

> **William Jovanovich,** 1920–2001
> publisher/writer

The only time I have trouble is when I'm right. Is it my fault it's so often?

> *The Miracle Worker*
> **William Gibson,** 1914–
> dramatist/writer

In the long course of history, having people who understand your thought is much greater security than another submarine.

J. William Fulbright, 1905–1995
U. S. senator, Arkansas

The last sound on the worthless earth will be two human beings trying to launch a homemade spaceship and already quarreling about where they are going next.

William Faulkner, 1897–1962
writer

The difference between fantasy and science fiction is that one has honest politicians, scrupulous lawyers, and altruistic doctors, while the other only has beings from outer space.

William John Watkins, 1942–
writer

After one look at this planet any visitor from outer space would say "I WANT TO SEE THE MANAGER."

The Adding Machine
William S. Burroughs, 1914–1997
writer

I confess freely to you, I could never look long upon a monkey, without very mortifying reflections.

William Congreve, 1670–1729
dramatist

Certain it is that no civilization can remain the highest if another civilization adds to the intelligence of its men the intelligence of its women.

William Isaac Thomas,
1863–1947
sociologist

The world is a looking-glass, and gives back to every man the reflection of his own face. Frown at it, and it will in turn look sourly upon you; laugh at it and with it, and it is a jolly kind companion.

Vanity Fair
William Makepeace Thackeray,
1811–1863
writer

When our first parents were driven out of Paradise, Adam is believed to have remarked to Eve: "My dear, we live in an age of transition."

William Ralph Inge, 1860–1954
priest/writer/educator

I feel like a fugitive from the law of averages.

Bill Mauldin, 1921–2003
editorial cartoonist

Had there been a computer a hundred years ago, it would probably have predicted by now there would be so many horse-drawn vehicles it would be impossible to clear up all the manure.

K. William Kapp, 1910–1976

economist

Rembrandt painted about 700 pictures—of these, 3,000 are in existence.

Wilhelm von Bode, 1845–1929

museum director

I am not an early riser. The self-respect which other men enjoy in rising early I feel due to me for waking up at all.

William Gerhardi, 1895–1977

writer/dramatist

I think it is much better for a book to have some parts that can be skipped just as well as not, you get through it so much faster. I have often thought what a good thing it would be if somebody would write a book that we could skip the whole of. I think a good many people would like to have such a book as that. I know I should.

William Henry Frost, 1863–1902
writer

With me a change of trouble is as good as a vacation.

William Lloyd George, 1927–
British peer/public relations and
advertising executive

The reason lightning doesn't strike twice in the same place is that the same place isn't there the second time.

Willie Tyler, 1940–
ventriloquist/comedian

America is the only country in the world that's still in the business of making bombs that can end the world, and TV shows that make it seem like a good idea.

Bill Maher, 1956–
comedian/pundit

I grabbed her by the lips and started biting her . . .

on how he invented cattle
"bulldogging"
Bill Pickett, 1870–1932
cowboy

I'm very appreciative of being indicted.

on being named to Florida Hall of
Fame
Bill Peterson, 1920–1993
football coach

My dad always told me the more you stomp in crap the worse it stinks.

Billy Ray Cyrus, 1961–
singer/songwriter/actor

Concentration-wise, we're having trouble crossing the line mentally from a toughness standpoint.

Bill Parcells, 1941–
football coach

Happiness is like a cat. If you try to coax it or call it, it will avoid you; it will never come. But if you pay no attention to it and go about your business, you'll find it rubbing against your legs and jumping into your lap.

William John Bennett, 1943–
politician/writer

I don't think there's anybody in this organization not focused on the 49ers—I mean Chargers.

Bill Belichick, 1952–
football coach

We give advice by the bucket, but take it by the grain.

William Rounseville Alger,
1822–1905
minister

We all like telling people what to do, which is perfectly all right except that most people do not like being told what to do.

J. William Fulbright, 1905–1995
U.S. senator, Arkansas

The pessimist complains about the wind; the optimist expects it to change; the realist adjusts the sails.

William Arthur Ward, 1921–1994
writer

In the evening
all the hours that weren't used
are emptied out
and the beggars are waiting to gather them up . . .

"Beggars and Kings"
W. S. Merwin, 1927–
poet

Coin Collection

"**N**ecessity, mother of invention," wrote playwright William Wycherly, probably under deadline to finish the second act . . . he also gave birth to the phrase "happy go lucky" and the word "nincompoop." Verbal inventiveness seems to be a talent shared with brother Bills.

"Variety's the very spice of life," William Cowper said in 1785—but instead of finding our own variations on the theme, we just repeat his. The irony would not be lost on the poet: he also wrote that "God moves in a mysterious way His wonders to perform . . . "

Film director Billy Wilder was the first to see—or at least say—that "hindsight is always 20/20." Shift focus to sixteenth-century poet Guillaume de Salluste

Du Bartas, who optimistically saw mankind "living hand to mouth," "marching cheek by jowl," and "in the jaws of death."

In 1916, newspaperman William Allen White said the Progressive Party was "all dressed up and nowhere to go." About 200 years earlier, dramatist William Congreve's fashion sense led him to advise, "Put your best foot foremost."

Gentleman Bill Miner, bank robber by trade, steals credit for the pithy "Hands up!" The singer William "Lefty" Frizzell wrote the equally covetous "If you've got the money, honey, I've got the time."

That line could be useful if you run for Congress someday. When your campaign calls for flag-waving, thank naval captain William Driver for being first to call the stars and stripes "Old Glory." Or recall general William Tecumseh Sherman, who famously turned down a GOP presidential pursuit with, "If drafted, I will not run; if nominated, I will not accept; if elected, I will not serve." Politics may have been purgatory to him, but he said, "War is hell."

But hold the fort (that's Sherman's, too): the most quoted writer in the English language was more than an unsurpassed playwright and poet. He also coined enough new words to circle the Globe, and some well-turned phrases we all speak trippingly off the tongue whether we know it or not. Yes, you're talking Shakespeare when you say:

Bag and baggage
Neither rhyme nor reason
Too much of a good thing
Laid on with a trowel
I have not slept one wink
To the manner born
That it should come to this

Sweets to the sweet
Exceedingly well read
Eaten me out of house and home
My heart's content
It was Greek to me
Forget and forgive
The milk of human kindness
A charmed life
One fell swoop
Love is blind
All that glisters is not gold
What the dickens
The world's mine oyster
As good luck would have it
A foregone conclusion
I will wear my heart upon my sleeve
The green-eyed monster
Neither here nor there

Wild-goose chase
I'll not budge an inch
For ever and a day
I have been in such a pickle
We have seen better days
Laugh yourself into stitches

five

Most Likely to Succeed

Be not afraid of greatness: some are born great, some achieve greatness and some have greatness thrust upon them.

> *Twelfth Night*
> **William Shakespeare,** 1564–1616
> dramatist/poet

Gentlemen, start your egos.

> hosting the *Seventy-Sixth Annual Academy Awards*
> **Billy Crystal,** 1948–
> actor/director

Live in terms of your strong points. Magnify them. Let your weaknesses shrivel up and die from lack of nourishment.

William Young Elliott, 1902–1997
poet

If some, we wonder, are selected to be the recipients of the gifts that lift humanity to its heights, can it be said that others are chosen to bear the burdens by which some balance may be struck?

William Trevor, 1928–
writer

When human power becomes so great and original that we can account for it only as a kind of divine imagination, we call it genius.

William Crashaw, 1572–1625
poet/clergyman

I would have picked up the artificial heart and thrown it on the floor and walked out and said he's dead if the press had not been there.

on first successful permanent
artificial heart transplant
William C. DeVries, 1943–
physician

I have always admired the ability to bite off more than one can chew and then chew it.

William C. deMille, 1878–1955
filmmaker/dramatist

It is from the top downward that culture filters. The Talented Tenth rises and pull all that are worth saving up to their vantage ground. This is the history of human progress.

W. E. B. DuBois, 1868–1963
educator/writer/historian

I don't even know why everyone else is here. They should just hand the gold medal to me. Everyone else can fight for second place.

at the 1984 Olympic games
Bill Johnson, 1960–
skier

Blow your own horn loud. If you succeed, people will forgive your noise; if you fail, they'll forget it.

William Feather, 1889–1981
publisher/writer

You've no idea what a poor opinion I have of myself—and how little I deserve it.

Ruddigore
Sir W. S. Gilbert, 1836–1911
lyricist/dramatist

Respectable men and women content with the good and easy living are missing some of the most important things in life. Unless you give yourself to some great cause you haven't even begun to live.

William Pierson Merrill,
1867–1954
minister

There are two kinds of adventurers: those who go truly hoping to find adventure and those who go secretly hoping they won't.

William Least Heat-Moon, 1940–
writer

A man must drive his energy, not be driven by it.

William Frederick Book,
1873–1940
psychologist

Who hasn't left the boat ramp at dawn and considered the endless possibilities of where to go and what might be accomplished?

Bill Dance, 1940–
angler

We are embarked as pioneers upon a new science and industry in which our problems are so new and unusual that it behooves no one to dismiss any novel idea with the statement, "It can't be done."

William E. Boeing, 1881–1956
aviation pioneer

When you are face to face with a difficulty, you are up against a discovery.

**William Thomson,
Lord Kelvin,** 1824–1907
mathematical physicist/engineer

Better that we should err in action than wholly refuse to perform. The storm is so much better than the calm, as it declares the presence of a living principle.

William Gilmore Simms,
1806–1870
writer

When you cannot make up your mind which of two evenly balanced courses of action you should take—choose the boldest.

W. J. Slim, 1891–1970
British army field marshall/Australian governor-general

If you pray for rain, don't grumble about the mud.

William Ward Ayer, 1892–1985
clergyman

If this life be not a real fight, in which something is eternally gained for the universe by success, it is no better than a game of private theatricals from which one may withdraw at will. But it feels like a real fight—as if there were something really wild in the universe which we, with all our idealities and faithfulnesses, are needed to redeem.

William James, 1842–1910
psychologist/philosopher

When you play against a stacked deck, make sure you've got a hand to beat theirs.

William Frederick "Buffalo Bill" Cody, 1846–1917
frontier scout/hunter/U.S. Army officer/showman

Adversity causes some men to break, others to break records.

William Arthur Ward, 1921–1994
writer

When a man is drowning, it may be better for him to try to swim than to thrash around waiting for divine intervention.

William Sloane Coffin, Jr.,
1924–2006
minister/activist

The world belongs to the Enthusiast who keeps cool.

William McFee, 1881–1966
writer

If you want to win a race you have to go a little berserk.

Bill Rodgers, 1947–
marathon runner

It's not my life, it's not my wife, so why worry?

> on staying cool in the clutch
> **Willie Davis,** 1940–
> baseball player

Once you've been tried and tested, there's a great confidence you get from being able to handle the heat.

> **William "Buck" Showalter,** 1956–
> baseball player/manager

No need for hope to get started, nor for success to persevere.

> **William I, "the Silent,"**
> 1533–1584
> prince of Orange

Let me tell you something, son,
Before you get much older,
You cannot hit the ball, my friend,
With the bat upon your shoulder.

Bill "the Singing Umpire" Byron,
1872–1955
baseball umpire

Everybody wants to go from A to B sitting down.

William S. "Big Bill" Knudsen,
1879–1948
U.S. Army general/automotive
executive

No pain, no palm; no thorns, no throne; no gall, no glory;
no cross, no crown.

William Penn, 1644–1718
founder of Pennsylvania colony

Defeat is worse than death because you have to live with defeat.

> **Bill Musselman,** 1940–2000
> basketball coach

Winning is an absurd and sophomoric enticement to a frazzled population. Winning to some means keeping the war going because that keeps the cash flowing in their direction. To others, winning means killing all the right people.

> on the "selling" of the Iraq War
> **Bill C. Davis,** 1951–
> dramatist/writer

Man is the only animal that laughs and weeps; for he is the only animal that is struck by the difference between what things are and what they might have been.

> **William Hazlitt,** 1778–1830
> essayist/critic

I am determined to sustain myself for as long as possible, and die like a soldier who never forgets what is due to his own honor and that of his country.

> **William B. Travis,** 1809–1836
> commander of Texas forces at the
> Alamo

If success is rare and slow, everybody knows how quick and easy ruin is.

> *Vanity Fair*
> **William Makepeace Thackeray,**
> 1811–1863
> writer

We're the only team in history that could lose nine games in a row and then go into a slump.

> **Bill Fitch,** 1934–
> basketball coach

Experience is a tough teacher. She gives the test first and the lesson after.

William H. Ottley, 1929–2005
skydiver/pilot

It is by attempting to reach the top in a single leap that so much misery is caused in the world.

William Corbett, 1680–1748
composer/musician

Defeat strips away false values and makes you realize what you really want. It stops you from chasing butterflies and puts you to work digging gold.

William Moulton Marston,
1893–1947
psychologist/comic book writer

If fate means you to lose, give him a good fight anyhow.

William McFee, 1881–1966
writer

Even Betty Crocker burns a cake now and then.

Bill Caudill, 1956–
baseball pitcher/coach

Some people are born slack—others have slacking thrust upon them.

Will Self, 1961–
writer

Nobody stands taller than those willing to stand corrected.

William Safire, 1929–
writer

The most important thing in life is not to capitalize on your gains. Any fool can do that. The really important thing is to profit from your losses. That requires intelligence; and it makes the difference between a man of sense and a fool.

William Bolitho, 1890–1930
writer

Falling short of perfection is a process that just never stops.

William Shawn, 1907–1992
editor

Public misbehavior by the famous is a powerful teaching tool.

Bill O'Reilly, 1949–
political commentator/broadcaster

Experience by itself teaches nothing; it must be coupled with theory, with profound knowledge.

William Edwards Deming,
1900–1993
statistician/productivity consultant

Experience is the great teacher; unfortunately, experience leaves mental scars, and scar tissue contracts.

William James "Will" Mayo,
1861–1939
physician/cofounder, the Mayo Clinic

The man whose first question, after what he considers to be a right course of action has presented itself, is "What will people say?" is not the man to do anything at all.

Sir William Arbuthnot-Lane,
1856–1943
physician

Decide promptly, but never give any reasons. Your decisions may be right, but your reasons are sure to be wrong.

William Murray, Lord Mansfield,
1705–1793
jurist

If you have built castles in the air, your work need not be lost; there is where they should be. Now put foundations under them.

William Graham Sumner,
1840–1910
educator/writer

As the essence of courage is to stake one's life on a possibility, so the essence of faith is to believe that the possibility exists.

William Salter, 1821–1910
minister

Never change a winning game; always change a losing one.

Bill Tilden, 1893–1953
tennis player

I've never wanted just part of the package, part of the prize. I want it all!

Bill McCartney, 1940–
football coach

I dare you, who think life is humdrum, to become involved. I dare you who are weak to become strong; you who are dull to be sparkling; you who are slaves to be kings.

William H. Danforth, 1870–1956
businessman

The biggest things are always the easiest to do because there is no competition.

Sir William Van Horne, 1843–1915
railway pioneer

O, what men dare do! what men may do! what men daily do, not knowing what they do!

Much Ado About Nothing
William Shakespeare, 1564–1616
dramatist/poet

Let every man who pants for fame select his own style of pant and go ahead.

Edgar Wilson "Bill" Nye,
1850–1896
journalist

Long before I was a star, I was a fan.

Bill Anderson, 1937–
singer/songwriter

There are times when someone on the street says, "Are you William Hurt?" and I will say, "No, not at the moment."

William Hurt, 1950–
actor

One must choose between Obscurity with Efficiency, and Fame with its inevitable collateral of Bluff.

William McFee, 1881–1966
writer

There's only a short walk from the hallelujah to the hoot.

William Kennedy, 1928–
writer

I cannot see why people are ashamed to acknowledge their passion for popularity. The love of popularity is the love of being beloved.

> **William Shenstone,** 1714–1763
> poet

I didn't know whether to check him or ask for his autograph.

> on opposing Wayne Gretzky
> **Bill Houlder,** 1967–
> hockey player

I may seem secure . . . I could have it made . . .
You might think you see a lucky man who made the grade.
Nobody knows what dreams I see
Ain't nobody really sure just who they wanna be . . .

> "Nobody Knows"
> **Billy Squier,** 1950–
> singer/songwriter

When the painting is finished, the subject reveals itself.

William Baziotes, 1912–1963
artist

True ambition is not what we thought it was. True ambition is the profound desire to live usefully and walk humbly under the grace of God.

William Griffith ("Bill W")
Wilson, 1895–1971
cofounder, Alcoholics Anonymous

Some folks are silly enough to have formed a plan to make a president of the U.S. out of this clerk and clod hopper.

William Henry Harrison,
1773–1841
U.S. president/governor, Indiana
territory/U.S. congressman/senator,
Ohio

Many people are thwarted by excessive ambition. They want a hundred thousand dollars but are unwilling to save a hundred dollars. They want a big house, but do not accumulate enough money to make the down payment on a small house. They want to write a book, but will not learn to write a letter. Most men become successful and famous, not through ambition, but through ability and character.

William Feather, 1889–1981
publisher/writer

Lady Luck has been good to me and I fancy she has been good to everyone. Only some people are dour, and when she gives them the come hither with her eyes, they look down or turn away and lift an eyebrow. But me, I give her the wink and away we go.

William Allen White, 1868–1944
newspaper editor/writer

I now perceive one immense omission in my Psychology—the deepest principle of Human Nature is the craving to be appreciated.

William James, 1842–1910
psychologist/philosopher

If at first you don't succeed, find out if the loser gets anything.

Bill Lyon, 1939–
sportswriter

Have I done the world good, or have I added a menace?

Guglielmo Marconi, 1874–1937
inventor/radio pioneer

Success is a lousy teacher. It seduces smart people into thinking they can't lose.

Bill Gates, 1955–
software architect/businessman/
philanthropist

What success I achieved in the theater is due to the fact that I have always worked just as hard when there were ten people in the house as when there were thousands. Just as hard in Springfield, Illinois, as on Broadway.

Bill "Bojangles" Robinson,
1878–1949
dancer

We have a lot of players in their first year. Some of them are also in their last year.

Bill Walsh, 1931–2007
football coach

Well, there are seven fielders in front of you, all of them placed so that they are in a position to pounce upon all kinds of drives, liners or grounders. The principal thing to do is to hit 'em where they ain't.

William Henry "Wee Willie" Keeler, 1872–1923
baseball player

In the world that we inhabit, having one hit is a lot better than having no hits.

William Shatner, 1931–
actor

When the consensus of scholarship says one thing and the Word of God another, the consensus of scholarship can go plumb to hell for all I care.

Billy Sunday, 1862–1935
baseball player/evangelist

Gettin' jiggy wit it, is like, the next level of cool. It's cool to the eighth power. Some people are fly, some people are kind of hot. But when you are the jiggiest, when you exude jiggy-essence, it's the acme of cool.

Will Smith, 1968–
actor/musician

I am, in point of fact, a particularly haughty and exclusive person, of pre-Adamite ancestral descent. You will understand this when I tell you that I can trace my ancestry back to a protoplasmal primordial atomic globule. Consequently, my family pride is something inconceivable.

The Mikado
Sir W. S. Gilbert, 1836–1911
lyricist/dramatist

There is no more reason to believe that man descended from an inferior animal than there is to believe that a stately mansion has descended from a small cottage.

Scopes "Monkey" Trial address
William Jennings Bryan,
1860–1925
lawyer/U.S. congressman, Nebraska/
U.S. secretary of state

Civilization is simply a series of victories over nature.

William Harvey, 1578–1657
physician

All modern men are descended from a worm-like creature, but it shows more on some people.

Will Cuppy, 1884–1949
humorist

A fire-mist and a planet,
A crystal and a cell,
A jellyfish and a saurian,
And caves where the cavemen dwell;
Then a sense of law and beauty,
And a face turned from the clod—
Some call it Evolution,
And others call it God.

"Each in His Own Tongue"
William Herbert Carruth,
1859–1924
poet

We came all this way to explore the moon, and the most important thing is that we discovered the earth.

Bill Anders, 1933–
U.S. Air Force officer/astronaut

I believe that man will not merely endure; he will prevail. He is immortal, not because he alone among creatures has an inexhaustible voice, but because he has a soul, a spirit capable of compassion and sacrifice and endurance.

William Faulkner, 1897–1962
writer

We are apt to say that money talks, but it speaks a broken, poverty-stricken language. Hearts talk better, clearer and with wider intelligence.

William Allen White, 1868–1944
newspaper editor/writer

Inquiry is human; blind obedience brutal. Truth never loses by the one but often suffers by the other.

William Penn, 1644–1718
founder of Pennsylvania colony

Whenever he saw a dollar in another man's hands he took it as a personal grudge, if he couldn't take it any other way.

The Gentle Grafter
William Sidney Porter (O. Henry),
1862–1910
writer

The barbarous gold barons—they did not find the gold, they did not mine the gold, they did not mill the gold, but by some weird alchemy all the gold belonged to them!

William D. "Big Bill" Haywood,
1869–1928
labor leader

Bring on the night, ring out the hour.
The days wear on but I endure.

Guillaume Apollinaire, 1880–1918
writer/art critic

Can anything be imagined more abhorrent to every sentiment of generosity or justice than the law which arms the rich with the legal right to fix, by assize, the wages of the poor? If this is not SLAVERY, we have forgotten the definition.

William Cullen Bryant, 1794–1878
poet/editor

If the State cannot survive the anti-slavery agitation, then let the State perish. If the Church must be cast down by the strugglings of Humanity to be free, then let the Church fall, and its fragments be scattered to the four winds of heaven, never more to curse the earth.

William Lloyd Garrison,
1805–1879
abolitionist/journalist

What has brought unique, irreplaceable me—out of all the possibilities of life—here, now, to this? Was all my youth— the paper route after school, the stolen moments in the back seats of borrowed cars, the football workouts, the cramming for finals—meant to end this way, dying in a muddy paddy?

William Broyles, Jr., 1944–
writer/editor/producer

The Hulk is the personification of the enemy which lurks under the surface of us all. We have to control that enemy within ourselves, or we can't control the conduct of the world.

on playing TV's Incredible Hulk
Bill Bixby, 1934–1993
actor/director

What lies behind us and what lies before us are tiny matters compared to what lies within us.

William Morrow, 1873–1931
publisher

There are two great days in a person's life—the day we are born and the day we discover why.

William Barclay, 1907–1978
writer/clergyman/educator

Singular Sensations

Greatness would not be remarkable if everyone were great. The irascibly unique actress Tallulah Bankhead seemed to agree when she said, "There have been only two geniuses in the world—Willie Mays and Willie Shakespeare."

But let's make room for the near-genius and the merely outstanding. Like Will Keith Kellogg, inventor of corn flakes, and William G. Morgan, who created volleyball; the two within three years of another in the 1890s.

The first combat jet plane was designed by Willy Messerschmitt; in peaceful skies, William Powell Lear founded the airplane company that bears executives and his name.

Billy Wilder won three Academy Awards in a single year: best picture, direction, and writing for *The Apartment*. Meanwhile, Bills and Wilhelms and their brothers have taken 21 Nobel Prizes. The youngest ever was William Henry Bragg, Jr., at 25. Cartoonist Bill Mauldin won his first Pulitzer at 23.

Good things are worth waiting for, though. At 54, Willie Shoemaker was the oldest jockey ever on the winning horse at the Kentucky Derby. Not fast enough for you? Bill France, Sr., was the brains behind the birth of NASCAR.

The future looks good; in his cult classic, *Neuromancer*, novelist William Gibson created the term *cyberspace*. (That's where you'll often find the wealthiest man in America, Bill Gates.)

six

Political
Animal

Fifty-four forty, or fight.

William Allen, 1803–1879
U.S. congressman/senator/governor,
Ohio

America is a land where a citizen will cross the ocean to fight for democracy—and won't cross the street to vote in a national election.

Bill Vaughan, 1915–1977
writer

Government by the people is possible, but highly improbable.

J. William Fulbright, 1905–1995
U.S. senator, Arkansas

The political machine triumphs because it is a united minority acting against a divided majority.

Will Durant, 1885–1981
philosopher/historian

Democracy is only an experiment in government, and it has the obvious disadvantage of merely counting votes instead of weighing them.

William Ralph Inge, 1860–1954
priest/writer/educator

In the end you must either allow people liberty or you must shoot them. If a man claims a vote you must either give him a vote or be prepared to take his life.

William Rees-Mogg, 1928–
journalist

Our elections are free; it's in the results where eventually we pay.

Bill Stern, 1907–1971
sportscaster

We are so concerned to flatter the majority that we lose sight of how often it is necessary, in order to preserve freedom for the minority, to face that majority down.

William F. Buckley, Jr., 1925–2008
writer/political commentator

People vote their resentment, not their appreciation.

William Bennett Munro,
1875–1957
social scientist

As long as I count the votes, what are you going to do about it?

William Marcy "Boss" Tweed,
1823–1878
politician

Bad politicians are sent to Washington by good people who don't vote.

William E. Simon, 1927–2000
U.S. treasury secretary

No politician can claim to be your average American, but some do a better job of faking it than others.

Bill Press, 1940–
political commentator/broadcaster

There's an easy way to run for most-liked in the class, and that's say yes. But if you want to legislate and be effective and do it right, you oftentimes have to say no.

Bill Thomas, 1941–
U.S. congressman, California

The Nation should have a tax system that looks like someone designed it on purpose.

William E. Simon, 1927–2000
U.S. treasury secretary

Think about it: We pay the government royalties in the form of taxes, for which it provides us with services. What is our capitalistic system but one big franchising deal?

William Rosenberg, 1916–2002
businessman

The administration says the American people want tax cuts. Well, duh. The American people also want drive-through nickel beer night. The American people want to lose weight by eating ice cream. The American people love the Home Shopping Network because it's commercial free.

Will Durst, 1952–
political satirist

Our differences are politics, our agreements principles.

William McKinley, 1843–1901
U.S. president/governor/U.S.
congressman, Ohio

In the United States grim poverty is a tragedy that great wealth makes a sin.

William Sloane Coffin, Jr.,
1924–2006
minister/activist

Love and business and family and religion and art and patriotism are nothing but shadows of words when a man's starving!

Heart of the West
William Sidney Porter (O. Henry),
1862–1910
writer

What are cherished principles for but to be violated in emergencies?

William Kristol, 1952–
political commentator/columnist

Real leadership is never arrogant. It is inspiring, it is positive, and it's strong—never blind or deaf to the world's concerns as we address our own.

> **Bill Richardson,** 1947–
> governor/U.S. congressman, New
> Mexico/U.N. ambassador/energy
> secretary

Experience suggests that the first rule of politics is never to say never. The ingenious human capacity for maneuver and compromise may make acceptable tomorrow what seems outrageous or impossible today.

> **William V. Shannon,** 1927–1988
> journalist/U.S. ambassador to Ireland

The American government is premised on the theory that if the mind of man is to be free, his ideas, his beliefs, his ideology, his philosophy must be placed beyond the reach of government.

William O. Douglas, 1898–1980
U.S. Supreme Court justice

When I want to buy up any politicians, I always find the anti-monopolists the most purchasable. They don't come so high.

William Henry Vanderbilt,
1821–1885
railway magnate

Power always has to be kept in check; power exercised in secret, especially under the cloak of national security, is doubly dangerous.

William Proxmire, 1915–2005
U.S. congressman, Wisconsin

That reminds me of the kind of politician who would chop down a tree, and then stand on the stump and give a speech about conservation.

Bill Bradley, 1943–
basketball player/U.S. senator,
New Jersey

. . . tell them the truth, then, not that power corrupts men; but men corrupt power.

The Recognitions
William Gaddis, 1922–1998
writer

We learn from history that we do not learn from history.

Georg Wilhelm Friedrich Hegel,
1770–1831
philosopher

There is nothing more corrupting, nothing more destructive of the noblest and finest feelings of our nature, than the exercise of unlimited power.

William Henry Harrison,
1773–1841
U.S. president/governor, Indiana
territory/U.S.congressman/senator,
Ohio

We look forward to the time when the Power of Love will replace the Love of Power.

William Ewart Gladstone,
1809–1898
British prime minister/chancellor
of the exchequer/member of
Parliament

All true trophies of the ages
Are from mother-love impearled;
For the hand that rocks the cradle
Is the hand that rules the world.

"What Rules the World"
William Ross Wallace, 1819–1881
poet

Those in power need checks and restraints lest they come to identify the common good for their own tastes and desires, and their continuation in office as essential to the preservation of the nation.

William O. Douglas, 1898–1980
U.S. Supreme Court justice

In politics, a lie unanswered becomes truth within 24 hours.

Willie Brown, 1934–
San Francisco mayor

We must not remember that Daniel Webster got drunk but only that he was a splendid constitutional lawyer. We must forget that George Washington was a slave owner, or that Thomas Jefferson had mulatto children, or that Alexander Hamilton had Negro blood, and simply remember the things we regard as creditable and inspiring. The difficulty, of course, with this philosophy is that history loses its value as an incentive and example; it paints perfect man and noble nations, but it does not tell the truth.

W. E. B. DuBois, 1868–1963
educator/writer/historian

Where there is no room for national pride or national shame about the past, there can be no national soul.

Sir William Patrick Deane, 1931–
jurist/governor-general of Australia

When public men indulge themselves in abuse, when they deny others a fair trial, when they resort to innuendo and insinuation, to libel, scandal, and suspicion, then our democratic society is outraged, and democracy is baffled.

J. William Fulbright, 1905–1995
U.S. senator, Arkansas

We have to live today by what truth we can get today and be ready tomorrow to call it falsehood.

William James, 1842–1910
psychologist/philosopher

If you ever live in a country run by a committee, be on the committee.

William Graham Sumner,
1840–1910
educator

Politics, when I am in it, it makes me sick.

William Howard Taft, 1857–1930
U.S. president/U.S. Supreme Court
chief justice

Necessity is the plea for every infringement of human freedom. It is the argument of tyrants; it is the creed of slaves.

William Pitt the Younger,
1759–1806
British prime minister/member of
Parliament

Democracy may not prove in the long run to be as efficient as other forms of government, but it has one saving grace: it allows us to know and say that it isn't.

Bill Moyers, 1934–
broadcast journalist

Men are apt to mistake the strength of their feeling for the strength of their argument. The heated mind resents the chill touch and relentless scrutiny of logic.

William Ewart Gladstone,
1809–1898
British prime minister/chancellor
of the exchequer/member of
Parliament

If the press is not free, if speech is not independent and untrammeled, if the mind is shackled or made impotent through fear, it makes no difference under what form of government you live, you are a subject and not a citizen.

William Edgar Borah, 1865–1940
U.S. senator, Idaho

One cannot always be sure of the truth of what one hears if he happens to be President of the United States.

William Howard Taft, 1857–1930
U.S. president/U.S. Supreme Court
chief justice

Without censorship, things can get terribly confused in the public mind.

William Westmoreland, 1914–2005
U.S. Army general/chief of staff

Here speaks a voice from America. The news may be good. The news may be bad. We shall tell you the truth.

first Voice of America broadcast to
Europe, February 24, 1942
William Harlan Hale, 1910–1974
writer/historian

We need more people speaking out. This country is not overrun with rebels and free thinkers. It's overrun with sheep and conformists.

Bill Maher, 1956–
comedian/pundit

Free speech is not to be regulated like diseased cattle and impure butter. The audience (in this case the judge or the jury) that hissed yesterday may applaud today, even for the same performance.

William O. Douglas, 1898–1980
U.S. Supreme Court justice

Continue to express your dissent and your needs, but remember to remain civilized, for you will sorely miss civilization if it is sacrificed in the turbulence of change.

Will Durant, 1885–1981
philosopher/historian

In a democracy dissent is an act of faith. Like medicine, the test of its value is not in its taste, but in its effects.

J. William Fulbright, 1905–1995
U.S. senator, Arkansas

Somewhere out there, beyond the walls of the courthouse, run currents and tides of public opinion which lap at the courtroom door.

William H. Rehnquist, 1924–2005
U.S. Supreme Court justice/chief
justice

It is in the nature of tyranny to deride the will of the people as the voice of the mob, and to denounce the cry for freedom as the roar of anarchy.

William Safire, 1929–
writer

The Press is at once the eye and the ear and the tongue of the people. It is the visible speech if not the voice of the democracy.

William Thomas Stead, 1849–1912
journalist

The fact is that there is a serious danger of this country becoming a pluto-democracy; that is, a sham republic with the real government in the hands of a small clique of enormously wealthy men, who speak through their money, and whose influence, even today, radiates to every corner of the United States.

William Gibbs McAdoo, 1863–1941
U.S. treasury secretary/Federal
Reserve Board chairman/senator,
California

Let the people think they govern, and they will be governed.

William Penn, 1644–1718
founder of Pennsylvania colony

Liberalism is trust of the people tempered by prudence. Conservatism is distrust of the people tempered by fear.

William Ewart Gladstone,
1809–1898
British prime minister/chancellor
of the exchequer/member of
Parliament

We have the power to do any damn fool thing we want to do, and we seem to do it about every ten minutes.

J. William Fulbright, 1905–1995
U.S. senator, Arkansas

Patriotism is the last refuge of scoundrels.

William Samuel Johnson,
1727–1819
statesman/U.S. senator, Connecticut

A politician will do anything to keep his job—even become a patriot.

William Randolph Hearst,
1863–1951
publisher/U.S. congressman,
New York

Like other idealisms, patriotism varies from a noble devotion to a moral lunacy.

William Ralph Inge, 1860–1954
priest/writer/educator

Best they honor thee
Who honor in thee only what is best.

Sir William Watson, 1858–1935
poet

. . . **a** grand revolution includes in it the sacrifice of one generation.

William Godwin, 1756–1836
writer/philosopher

Men do not fight for flag or country, for the Marine Corps or glory or any other abstraction. They fight for one another.

William Manchester, 1922–2004
writer/historian

You cannot qualify war in harsher terms than I will. War is cruelty, and you cannot refine it; and those who brought war into our country deserve all the curses and maledictions a people can pour out.

William Tecumseh Sherman,
1820–1891
U.S. Army general

The surest way to become a pacifist is to join the infantry.

Bill Mauldin, 1921–2003
editorial cartoonist

I know and all the world knows, that revolutions never go backwards.

William Henry Seward, 1801–1872
governor/U.S. senator, New York/U.S.
secretary of state

If a nation ambitious for universal conquest gets off to a flying start in a war of the future, it may be able to control the whole world more easily than a nation has controlled a continent in the past.

Billy Mitchell, 1879–1936
U.S. Army general/military aviation
pioneer

There is one certain means by which I can be sure never to see my country's ruin—I will die in the last ditch.

William I, 1772–1843
king of the Netherlands

Gentlemen, let us ever remember that our interest is in concord, not in conflict; and that our real eminence rests in the victories of peace, not those of war.

William McKinley, 1843–1901
U.S. president/governor/U.S.
congressman, Ohio

I gave my life for freedom—this I know:
For those who bade me fight had told me so.

"Five Souls"
William Norman Ewer, 1885–1976
journalist

The choice is no longer between Utopia and the pleasant ordered world that our fathers knew. The choice is between Utopia and Hell.

William Henry Beveridge,
1879–1963
economist

We are beginning to resemble extinct dinosaurs, who suffered from too much armor and too little brain.

William Sloane Coffin, Jr.,
1924–2006
minister/activist

Since there will be no one left to talk peace after the next war, it makes good sense to break with tradition and hold the peace conference first.

William Glasser, 1925–
psychiatrist

It is the exclusive province of Congress to change a state of peace into a state of war.

> **William Paterson,** 1745–1806
> governor, New Jersey/U.S. Supreme
> Court justice

I rejoice that America has resisted. Three millions of people, so dead to all the feelings of liberty, as voluntarily to submit to be slaves, would have been fit instruments to make slaves of the rest.

> **William Pitt the Elder,**
> **Lord Chatham,** 1708–1778
> British secretary of state/prime
> minister

Remorse begets reform.

> **William Cowper,** 1731–1800
> poet

It is pretty evident what will be my fate. I have done much to prosecute the contest, and one thing I have done, which the British will never pardon—I have signed the Declaration of Independence. I shall be hung.

William Williams, 1731–1811
Continental Congress delegate,
Connecticut

After an American has been in a totalitarian country for several months, he is greatly relieved when he reaches home. He feels that bonds have been released and that he is free. He can speak above a whisper, and he walks relaxed and unguarded as though he were no longer being followed. After a recent trip I said to a neighbor, "It's wonderful to be back in a nation where even a riot may be tolerated."

William O. Douglas, 1898–1980
U.S. Supreme Court justice

Protectionism is the ally of isolationism, and isolationism is the Dracula of American foreign policy.

William G. Hyland, 1929–2008
editor/writer/U.S. deputy national
security advisor

One difference between French appeasement and American appeasement is that France pays ransom in cash and gets its hostages back while the United States pays ransom in arms and gets additional hostages taken.

William Safire, 1929–
writer

Remember, the German people are the chosen of God. On me, the German Emperor, the spirit of God has descended. I am His sword, His weapon, and His vice-regent.

Wilhelm II, 1859–1941
German emperor

The destiny of the American people is to subdue the continent—to rush over this vast field to the Pacific Ocean . . . to change darkness into light and confirm the destiny of the human race. . . . Divine task! Immortal mission!

William Gilpin, 1724–1804
minister/artist/writer

If survival is the top priority—and I can think of nothing else on which we could more easily agree among religions, ideologies and scientific viewpoints—then the preservation of world peace is our most important objective, dominating all others.

Willy Brandt, 1913–1992
West German chancellor

To become a great man it is necessary to be a great rascal.

Guillaume Dubois, 1656–1723
cardinal/statesman

Justice delayed is justice denied.

William Ewart Gladstone,
1809–1898
British prime minister/chancellor
of the exchequer/member of
Parliament

Who thinks the law has anything to do with justice? It's what
we have because we can't have justice.

Laidlaw
William McIlvanney, 1936–
writer

Government was intended to suppress injustice, but its effect
has been to embody and perpetuate it.

William Godwin, 1756–1836
writer/philosopher

When we talk about justice in America we're really talking about justice brought about by the people, not by judges who are tools of the establishment or prosecutors who are equally tools of the establishment or the wardens or the police officers.

William Kunstler, 1919–1995
lawyer/activist

If to be feelingly alive to the sufferings of my fellow-creatures is to be a fanatic, I am one of the most incurable fanatics ever permitted to be at large.

William Wilberforce, 1759–1833
abolitionist/British member of
Parliament

When liberty destroys order, the hunger for order will destroy liberty.

Will Durant, 1885–1981
philosopher/historian

I found myself in racial situations for which I, as a person of a different race, had no frame of reference. I sensed the tension created by always being on guard, by never totally relaxing. I felt the pain of racial arrogance directed my way. I knew the loneliness of being white in a black world. And I realized how much I will never know about what it is to be black in America.

Bill Bradley, 1943–
basketball player/U.S. senator,
New Jersey

God of justice, save the people
From the clash of race and creed,
From the strife of class and faction,
Make our nation free indeed.

"Not Alone for Mighty Empire"
William Pierson Merrill,
1867–1954
minister

Prisoner, God has given you good abilities, instead of which you go about the country stealing ducks.

William Saint Julien Arabin,
1773–1841
jurist

O ye who lead,
Take heed!
Blindness we may forgive, but baseness we will smite.

"An Ode in Time of Hesitation"
William Vaughn Moody, 1869–1910
poet/dramatist

Everybody has a little bit of Watergate in him.

Billy Graham, 1918–
evangelist

I proclaim that all ye Pilgrims do gather at ye meeting house, there to listen to ye Pastor and render Thanksgiving to ye Almighty God for all his blessings.

William Bradford, 1590–1657
governor, Plymouth colony,
Massachusetts

Bill's the One

There have been enough kings and emperors to fill Europe's churchyards; plenty of prime ministers; six signers of the Declaration of Independence; eleven U.S. attorneys general; eleven Supreme Court justices; and four U.S. presidents.

And there have been some also-rans: at least three little-known Bills have thrown their hats in the ring for a chance to move into the White House—the place Bill Clinton called either "the finest public housing in America or the crown jewel of the penal system."

In 1960 it was time—someone thought—for counter-culture bookstore owner Bill Smith: he was nominated at the convention of the Beat Party of America, held in a Greenwich Village nightclub.

Baseball star Bill "The Spaceman" Lee launched himself into political orbit in 1988 as candidate of the Canadian Political Rhinoceros party, with the motto, "No guns. No butter. Both can kill." The CPR to the rescue.

But it was Oklahoma's William "Alfalfa Bill" Murray, opposing FDR for the Democratic nomination in 1932, whose footnote in history includes this slogan: "Bread, Butter, Bacon, and Beans." And they say electioneering is all hot air.

seven

Seven Ages of
Bill

In the early days of the Indian Territory, there were no such things as birth certificates. You being there was certificate enough.

Will Rogers, 1879–1935
humorist/actor

Nature makes boys and girls lovely to look upon so they can be tolerated until they acquire some sense.

William Lyon Phelps, 1865–1943
writer/educator

This is the beginning of sadness, I say to myself,
as I walk through the universe in my sneakers.
It is time to say good-bye to my imaginary friends,
time to turn the first big number.

"On Turning Ten"
Billy Collins, 1941–
poet

Youth should be radical. Youth should demand change in the world. Youth should not accept the old order if the world is to move on. But the old orders should not be moved easily— certainly not at the mere whim or behest of youth. There must be clash and if youth hasn't enough force or fervor to produce the clash the world grows stale and stagnant and sour in decay.

William Allen White, 1868–1944
newspaper editor/writer

It is a point of pride for the American male to keep the same size jockey shorts for his entire life.

Bill Cosby, 1937–
actor/writer/producer

My heart leaps up when I behold
A rainbow in the sky:
So was it when my life began;
So is it now I am a man;
So be it when I shall grow old,
Or let me die!
The Child is father of the Man;
I could wish my days to be
Bound each to each by natural piety.

"My Heart Leaps Up When I Behold"
William Wordsworth, 1770–1850
poet

I don't want to achieve immortality by being inducted into the Hall of Fame. I want to achieve immortality by not dying.

William de Morgan, 1839–1917
artist

Society at its best cannot live apart from the touch of the living multitude. It lives by being born again and again in the children of every generation.

William Lowe Bryan, 1860–1955
educator

Grow up as soon as you can. It pays. The only time you really live fully is from thirty to sixty. . . . The young are slaves to dreams; the old servants of regrets.

William Hervey Allen, 1889–1949
writer

Childhood is a disease—a sickness that you grow out of.

William Golding, 1911–1993
writer

The reveries of youth, in which so much energy is wasted, are the yearnings of a Spirit made for what it has not found but must forever seek as an Ideal

William Ellery Channing,
1780–1842
theologian

Youth should heed the older-witted
When they say, don't go too far—
Now their sins are all committed,
Lord, how virtuous they are!

"Pious Helen"
Wilhelm Busch, 1832–1908
artist/poet

You can't talk about heartbreak to a kid.

Will Eisner, 1917–2005
comic book artist/writer/publisher

Kids: they dance before they learn there is anything that isn't music.

William Stafford, 1914–1993
poet

There have always been grievances and youth has always been the agitator.

William O. Douglas, 1898–1980
U.S. Supreme Court justice

They're going to retire my uniform . . . with me still in it.

Billy Conigliaro, 1947–
baseball player

I look at the kids over here and the way they're playing and the way they're fighting for themselves, and that says one thing to me: "Willie, say goodbye to America."

on his 1973 retirement
Willie Mays, Jr., 1931–
baseball player

Life begins at 40—but so do fallen arches, rheumatism, faulty eyesight, and the tendency to tell a story to the same person, three or four times.

William Feather, 1889–1981
publisher/writer

First your legs go. Then you lose your reflexes. Then you lose your friends.

Willie Pep, 1922–2006
boxer

The past is never dead, it is not even past.

Requiem for a Nun
William Faulkner, 1897–1962
writer

You'll find as you grow older that you weren't born such a very great while ago after all.

William Dean Howells, 1837–1920
writer

It's been so long now, but it seems now that it was only
   yesterday.
Gee, ain't it funny, how time slips away.

"Funny How Time Slips Away"
Willie Nelson, 1933–
singer/songwriter

I have enough money to last me the rest of my life—provided I die tomorrow.

Bill Fitch, 1934–
basketball coach

Time is a storm in which we are all lost.

William Carlos Williams,
1883–1963
poet/physician

I recently turned fifty, which is young for a tree, midlife for an elephant, and ancient for a quarter-miler, who's son now says, "Dad, I just can't run the quarter with you anymore unless I bring something to read."

Bill Cosby, 1937–
actor/writer/producer

Though I look old, yet I am strong and lusty,
For in my youth I never did apply
Hot and rebellious liquors in my blood,
Nor did not with unbashful forehead woo
The means of weakness and debility.
Therefore my age is as a lusty winter,
Frosty, but kindly.

As You Like It
William Shakespeare, 1564–1616
dramatist/poet

I surely wouldn't want to grow younger. The older you become, the more you know; your bank account of knowledge is much richer.

William Holden, 1918–1981
actor

A man of fifty looks as old as Santa Claus to a girl of twenty.

William Feather, 1889–1981
publisher/writer

... **S**till, it's a gift,
at forty-five to run, much less run good,
and look far newer than a classic should.

"Dividing Classics from Antiques"
William John Watkins, 1942–
writer

I'll borrow life, and not grow old.

Ionica
William Johnson Cory, 1823–1892
educator/poet

There's this guy on the team who's grumpy. And he'll be grumpy when he's old. But not me. When I'm old, I'll be fat and happy.

William "The Refrigerator" Perry, 1962–
football player

I wish I could have known earlier that you have all the time you'll need right up to the day you die.

William T. Wiley, 1937–
artist

God put me on this earth to accomplish a certain number of things. Right now I am so far behind that I will never die.

Calvin and Hobbes
Bill Watterson, 1958–
cartoonist

It's never safe to be nostalgic about something until you're absolutely certain there's no chance of its coming back.

Bill Vaughan, 1915–1977

writer

Oh why should the spirit of mortal be proud?
Like a fast-flitting meteor, a fast-flying cloud,
A flash of the lightning, a break of the wave,
He passes from life to his rest in the grave.

"Mortality"
William Knox, 1789–1825
poet

Men fear death, as if unquestionably the greatest evil, and yet no man knows that it may not be the greatest good.

William Mitford, 1744–1827
historian

If I were a Tibetan priest and ate everything perfect, maybe I'd live to be 105. The way I'm going now, I'll probably only make it to 102. I'll give away three years to beer.

Bill "The Spaceman" Lee, 1946–
baseball player

Everybody has got to die, but I always believed an exception would be made in my case. Now what?

William Saroyan, 1908–1981
writer

I'm checking for loopholes.

reading the Bible, shortly before his death
W. C. Fields, 1880–1946
actor/comedian

Then there were the wits,
using their last breath to exhale a line,
a devastating capper, as if the world
were simply a large gallery buzzing with people,
and now it was time to throw on a long scarf
and make an exit, leaving
it to someone else to close the door.

"Death Bed"
Billy Collins, 1941–
poet

You living friends who pass me by
As you are now, so once was I
As I am now, so you must be
Prepare for death and follow me

gravestone inscription
William Kidd, 1645–1701
sailor/privateer

I now have no time to be tired.

> last words
> **Wilhelm I,** 1797–1888
> German emperor

So live, that when thy summons comes to join
The innumerable caravan which moves
To that mysterious realm where each shall take
His chamber in the silent halls of death,
Thou go not, like the quarry-slave at night,
Scourged to his dungeon, but sustained and soothed
By an unfaltering trust, approach thy grave
Like one that wraps the drapery of his couch
About him, and lies down to pleasant dreams.

> "Thanatopsis"
> **William Cullen Bryant,** 1794–1878
> poet/editor

When my obituary notice at last appears in the *Times*, and they say: "What, I thought he died years ago," my ghost will gently chuckle.

W. Somerset Maugham, 1874–1965
writer/dramatist

Those blessings of our early youth
Shall cheer our latest age.

"The Doves"
William Cowper, 1731–1800
poet

One trouble with growing older is that it gets progressively tougher to find a famous historical figure who didn't amount to much when he was your age.

Bill Vaughan, 1915–1977
writer

The view after seventy is breathtaking. What is lacking is someone, anyone, of the older generation to whom you can turn when you want to satisfy your curiosity about some detail of the landscape of the past. There is no longer any older generation. You have become it, while your mind was mostly on other matters.

Billie Dyer and Other Stories
William Keepers Maxwell, Jr.,
1908–2000
editor/writer

The belief that youth is the happiest time of life is founded on a fallacy. The happiest person is the person who thinks the most interesting thoughts, and we grow happier as we grow older.

William Lyon Phelps, 1865–1943
writer/educator

The stately ship is seen no more,
The fragile skiff attains the shore;
And while the great and wise decay,
And all their trophies pass away,
Some sudden thought, some careless rhyme,
Still floats above the wrecks of Time.

"On an Old Song"
William Edward Hartpole Lecky,
1838–1903
historian/poet

And yet the wiser mind
Mourns less for what age takes away,
Than what it leaves behind.

"The Fountain"
William Wordsworth, 1770–1850
poet

It is my aim, and every effort bent, that the sum and history of my life, which in the same sentence is my obit and epitaph too, shall be them both: He made the books and he died.

William Faulkner, 1897–1962
writer

That is no country for old men. The young
In one another's arms, birds in the trees—
Those dying generations—at their song.

"Sailing to Byzantium"
William Butler Yeats, 1865–1939
poet/dramatist

I hate to see that evenin' sun go down . . .

"St. Louis Blues"
W. C. Handy, 1873–1958
musician/composer

No funeral gloom, my dears, when I am gone,
Corpse-gazings, tears, black raiment, graveyard grimness;
Yours still, you mine, remember all the best
Of our past moments, and forget the rest,
And so, to where I wait, come gently on.

William Allingham: A Diary
William Allingham, 1824–1889
poet

We are temporary organs of the race, cells in the body of life; we die and drop away that life may remain young and strong. If we were to live forever, growth would be stifled, and youth would find no room on earth. Death, like style, is the removal of rubbish, the circumcision of the superfluous. In the midst of death life renews itself immortally.

Will Durant, 1885–1981
philosopher/historian

Trust flattering life no more, redeem time past,
And live each day as if it were thy last.

"Death's Last Will"
**William Drummond, of
Hawthornden,** 1585–1649
poet

The living was the prize;
The ending's not the story.

"Goodbye"
William Finn, 1952–
songwriter

Index of Names